THE BIG 5

Discovering the Five Foundations Every Christian
Should Know!

Daniel B. Gilbert, Ph.D.

2

Copyright © 2017 by **Daniel B. Gilbert, Ph.D.**

All rights reserved. No part of this publication may be reproduced, distributed or transmitted in any form or by any means, without prior written permission.

Scripture quotations marked (ESV) are taken from The ESV® Bible (The Holy Bible, English Standard Version®) copyright © 2001 by Crossway, a publishing ministry of Good News Publishers. ESV® Text Edition: 2011. The ESV® text has been reproduced in cooperation with and by permission of Good News Publishers. Unauthorized reproduction of this publication is prohibited. Used by permission. All rights reserved.

Scripture quotations marked (NASB) are taken from the New American Standard Bible ® (NASB), copyright © 1960, 1962, 1963, 1968, 1971, 1972, 1973, 1975, 1977, 1995 by The Lockman Foundation. Used by permission. www.Lockman.org.

Scripture quotations marked (NIV) are taken from the Holy Bible, New International Version. Copyright © 1973, 1978, 1984, 2011 by Biblica, Inc.® Used by permission. All rights reserved worldwide.

Scripture quotations marked (NKJV) are taken from the New King James Version®. Copyright © 1982 by Thomas Nelson, Inc. Used by permission. All rights reserved.

Scripture quotations marked (NLT) are taken from the Holy Bible, New Living Translation, copyright © 1996, 2004, 2007 by Tyndale House Foundation. Used by permission of Tyndale House Publishers, Inc., Carol Stream, Illinois 60188. All rights reserved.

"In Christ Alone" lyrics by Stuart Townend and Keith Getty Copyright © 2002 Thankyou Music (PRS) (adm. Worldwide at CapitalCMGPublishing.com excluding Europe which is adm. by Intergritymusic.com) All rights reserved. Used by permission.

All reasonable efforts have been made to contact the copyright holders.

Sermon to Book
www.sermontobook.com

The Big 5: Discovering the Five Foundations Every Christian Should Know / Daniel B. Gilbert, Ph.D.
ISBN-13: 978-1-945793-13-4
ISBN-10: 1-945793-13-9

"What a *timely* book! What a *needed* book! ... Danny is an outstanding, reverent and accurate teacher of God's Word. ... He correctly sees a gaping hole in the body of Christ that needs to be addressed, *now*. ... My prayer is that *many* will read *The Big 5* and adopt what he expertly communicates in it. Please share this with others!"

—Brad Matthew Abley, M.Div., Pastor, Author, and Religious Broadcaster

"As one who believes strongly that Christians are called to influence civic society and the broader culture, I believe Dr. Gilbert's book, *The Big 5* is essential reading for today's Christians. Dr. Gilbert explores what he calls "the Big 5" doctrines that will help readers become grounded in sound doctrine and therefore be better equipped to stand firm in their Christian faith in ever-shifting and even hostile cultures. I have known Daniel for over 28 years and he has been true to God and an articulate defender of sound Christian theology. I encourage believers to read his book to grow stronger in the foundations of the Christian faith."

—Ralph Reed, Ph.D., Founder and Chairman, Faith and Freedom Coalition

"*The Big 5* lays down influential stones of spiritual truth in a time of moral relevance. Daniel Gilbert provides the underpinnings from which a strong structure of lifelong faith can be built upon God's word. His dedication as a theologian, his experience as a pastor, and his daily walk of prayer and study of God's word are exemplified by his utter dependence on the ministry of the Holy Spirit. *The Big 5* is a must-read for strengthening your core understanding of God's word and provides a practical pathway to a dynamic walk and relationship with Jesus!"

—John Tayloe, President, Strategic Communications Group

"I believe *The Big 5* is a solid primer on the essentials of the faith as framed by the Reformation, and Luther in particular. Dr. Gilbert has developed a meaningful and helpful focus for times like these when we need to know in Whom we believe and be able to articulate the essentials that make our belief in Jesus understandable and, hopefully, unshakable."

—David Gyterson, Ph.D., Associate Provost/Dean Beeson Center at Asbury Theological Seminary and Professor of Leadership Formation and Renewal

"In *The Big 5*, Dr. Daniel Gilbert does what he does best, which is to communicate the treasures of the Reformation in a way that is passionate, insightful, and clarifying. Dr. Gilbert throws dazzling light on the teachings of the reformers, and warns of the various ways in which their insights are in danger of being lost in the modern church. Drink from this well, reader, and be refreshed!"

—Michael J. Chan, Ph.D., US Naval Officer and Former Assistant Professor of Old Testament, Luther Seminary

"From the opening paragraph, I wanted to read more and I wanted to read quickly. ... This is a book all evangelical churches should make available to their members; and I think the "old truths made new" contained within the book ... should be read at least once a year. It is an excellent and timely reminder on where we base our faith: the word of God and the life, death and resurrection of His son Jesus Christ. Sadly, in many cases the church has lost its way. This book seeks to bring us back to where the truth lies."

—Phil Smith, Elder and Businessman, Aberdeen, Scotland

"I believe Dr. Gilbert's book will enlighten and set lukewarm believers on fire and strengthen all believers in their faith.... If I were alone in paradise, I would only need my Holy Bible and a copy of *The Big 5* to feed my soul. [*The Big 5*] is a GPS that keeps us on course, steering us away from half-truths, idols, and misinformation. It is a true gyroscope for "God's Positioning System.""

—Deacon Charles Johnson, Bel Air Presbyterian Church, Los Angeles, CA

To the love of my life, Mary Beth, who has encouraged and supported me to write this book. I am so grateful for all her sacrifice and patience with me.

I also dedicate this work to my late spiritual father and mentor, Professor J. Rodman Williams, Ph.D. I am forever thankful for your mentorship of over nineteen years, your love for God, sound theology, and for making me your "son of the faith." Without you, I would not have fallen in love with theology and pursued further education and ministry.

CONTENTS

Note from the Author

Hello, and thank you for purchasing *The Big Five*.

I wrote *The Big Five* so that every Christian can discover or rediscover some of the main doctrines and foundations of the Christian faith. It is my desire to help you and others understand how important these foundations are for believers.

Therefore, accompanying each chapter of the book is a set of reflective questions. These workbook sections serve as a practical tool to help you get the most out of the book—to help you truly understand and learn to apply the fundamental doctrines of our faith as found in God's Word.

Each workbook section includes questions for discussion or reflection as well as a practical action step. I recommend you go through these sections with a pen in order to write your thoughts in the areas provided.

Whether you go through the questions on your own, with a friend, or with a small group, it is my hope that you will have a greater understanding of the Christian faith. I also hope you will thoroughly enjoy the book, grow from the experience, and then share it with a friend!

INTRODUCTION

The Big 5

What you heard from me, keep as the pattern of sound teaching, with faith and love in Christ Jesus. — 2 Timothy 1:13 (NIV)

The Big 5 is a phrase that may bring to mind a number of images. The most obvious is college football, but it also refers to five animals common to Africa: the lion, the elephant, the rhinoceros, the Cape buffalo, and one that is rarely seen, the leopard. This phrase also identifies a popular sporting goods chain store, Big 5.

If the church forgets these most important Big 5, it will begin to lose direction, hope, foundation, and ultimately its impact on the world.

And let's not forget that many in the business world believe that to be successful, one must play an active part in the Big 5 of social media: Facebook, Twitter, Google, LinkedIn, and Instagram.

However, there is a different Big 5 that relates to the importance of sound theology and doctrine.

See, if a business does not actively use the big five in social media, it will likely be left behind. In the same way, if the church forgets these most important Big 5, it will begin to lose direction, hope, foundation, and, ultimately, its impact on the world, which already seems to be happening.

In an age when many people, even Christians, don't seem to care about the truth revealed in God's Word, having a renewed understanding of the Big 5 is crucial.

The Big 5 of our faith were foundational for centuries in keeping the church focused on sound doctrine and theology.

The Big 5 of our faith are doctrines that were developed and clarified during the Reformation period of the church in the 1500s. For centuries, they were foundational in keeping the Protestant church focused on sound doctrine and theology. So what are the Big 5?

1. *Sola scriptura*: Scripture alone is authoritative over all areas of a Christian's life.

2. *Solus Christus*, or *Solo Christo*: Christ alone is Lord and Savior and provides salvation.
3. *Sola gratia*: Salvation is by grace alone.
4. *Sola fide*: Righteousness is by faith alone.
5. *Soli deo gloria*: For the glory of God alone.

The Lord does not change, nor do the doctrines rooted in His Word. However, in the past one hundred years or so, the mainstream church has accelerated further away from the Big 5 of our faith. Culture has negatively affected the church, instead of the church influencing culture.

My hope for you is that this book helps you—helps *us*—reverse that course.

Introduction Notes

CHAPTER ONE

A New Reformation

As I urged you when I went into Macedonia, stay there in Ephesus so that you may command certain people not to teach false doctrines any longer or to devote themselves to myths and endless genealogies. — 1 Timothy 1:3-4 (NIV)

It is absolutely imperative that we rediscover the foundations of our faith and that we understand the signs of the times. Christians need to be assured of what they believe. They must be confident and equipped to share it with the world.

The Protestant Reformation

The Reformation "officially" began on October 31, 1517, when Martin Luther, a professor of theology, nailed his Ninety-Five Theses on the door of Castle Church in Wittenberg, Germany. These propositions challenged the religious establishment by renouncing the false teaching, corrupt doctrines, and pagan practices of the Roman Catholic Church.

> *The Church had imposed oppressive rituals and rules on the people, which prevented them from truly knowing and experiencing God.*

For centuries, the Roman Catholic Church had been moving away from faithfully preaching and teaching the Word of God. It had imposed oppressive rituals and rules on the people, which prevented them from truly knowing and experiencing God.

At that time in Europe, a parish church was established over a certain locality. The parish priest was required to visit and minister to all of the families in his parish. Bishops who were in charge of the entire region began to purchase their positions, which were called *bishoprics.* But priests had stopped performing their pastoral duties, such as administering last rites. Because of this, church members did not feel as though their priests were caring for them.

On top of that, priests had begun to sell indulgences. Church members were encouraged to pay money to the church to receive forgiveness for their sins—and additional money for forgiveness of any future sins—to prevent time spent in purgatory.

Not including their regular giving to the church, this amounted to approximately half of the people's annual salary.

The Roman Catholic Church was in the process of building St. Peter's Basilica in Rome and was running short of money, so selling indulgences helped fund the project.

It was nothing more than a tax scam.

People were finally able to read or hear the Bible preached in their own language, rather than in the traditional Latin. Not surprisingly, people began to realize the truth.

Father Tetzel was one of the leaders in charge of selling indulgences during this time. The following quote from Tetzel reveals how deceitful this doctrine was: "As soon as the coin in the coffer rings, the soul out of purgatory springs."[1]

Many people were aware of the rampant corruption and had grown extremely frustrated. With the invention of the Gutenberg Press in 1440, people were finally able to read or hear the Bible preached in their own language, rather than in the traditional Latin. Not surprisingly, people began to realize the truth.

Prior to the invention of the printing press, the Bible was written only in Latin (the Vulgate), a language unknown to common, uneducated people of the time.

Sermons were also preached in Latin, so most churchgoers didn't understand what the priest was communicating. Priests would turn their backs to the people during Holy Communion, repeating mysterious-seeming phrases in Latin. According to the priests, something mystical happened while repeating these phrases; they claimed that the bread and wine literally turned into the body and blood of Jesus Christ. This belief became known as transubstantiation. Of course, nobody could read the Bible and examine Scripture to determine if this teaching on holy communion was true or not.

People heard these messages focused on the Big 5 of our faith, and something began to stir in their hearts.

People began holding church meetings in their homes—usually wealthy people because they could read the Bible and other Christian writings. The messages of Martin Luther and other reformers began to circulate. People heard these messages that focused on the Big 5 of our faith, and something began to stir in their hearts.

The invention of the printing press only stoked the fire of frustration already sparking in the church. It was as if God were saying, "Now is the time for spreading the Word of Truth and information." God's people wanted to know the truth.

Steven Ozment, a scholar on the Reformation period, wrote of this need for information: "The failure of the late medieval church to provide a theology and spirituality that could satisfy and discipline religious hearts and minds was the most important religious precondition of the Protestant Reformation."[2]

Soon, people began to teach against many regular Church practices, such as prayers to the saints, relic worship, and common errors in interpreting the Scriptures.

The doctrines these reformers taught weren't new; they were simply returning to what Jesus and the apostles had taught about the Christian faith.

God used Martin Luther to set the stage for a spiritual reformation. There were many others God used during this period of time, such as Martin Bucer, Philip Melanchthon, John Calvin, and later John Knox. These men communicated that freedom from sin comes from belief in Jesus Christ alone. They focused on the authority of the Holy Scriptures rather than on Church authority. In their minds, it was time for the Church to submit to God's Word.

The Reformation set the stage for the global church to grow exponentially over the next four hundred years. Yet the doctrines these reformers taught were not new; they were simply returning to what Jesus and the apostles had taught about the Christian faith.

False Doctrine Within the Modern-Day Church

False teaching and erroneous doctrine had crept into the early church in Ephesus. Young Timothy, Paul's closest disciple, had taken over leadership of this church for Paul. In his letter to Timothy, Paul wrote of his concerns for the church: "The Spirit clearly says that in later times some will abandon the faith and follow deceiving spirits and things taught by demons" (1 Timothy 4:1 NIV).

Just like the first-century church and the Roman Catholic Church prior to the Reformation, many modern-day churches and denominations are teaching false doctrines.

I believe we are in those latter times, and the worldwide church needs to open its eyes. Since the church's inception, Satan has tried to lull it to sleep. Paul knew this would happen, which is why he warned Timothy that many would abandon the faith to follow "deceiving spirits and things taught by demons."

Paul's letter to the Galatians revealed that deception had also seeped into the church at Galatia. Paul was astonished that the church had so quickly turned to a different gospel, which in his mind was no gospel at all. He wrote, "Evidently some people are throwing you into confusion and are trying to pervert the gospel of Christ. But even if we or an angel from heaven should preach a gospel other than the one we preached to you, let them be under God's curse!" (Galatians 1:7-8 NIV).

Paul emphatically repeated: "If anybody is preaching to you a gospel other than what you accepted, let them be under God's curse!" (Galatians 1:9 NIV). He was deeply concerned for the state of the church.

The devil, whose goal is to prevent people from knowing and understanding the truth of Jesus Christ, has twisted Scripture and deceived God's people.

Just like the first-century church and the Roman Catholic Church prior to the Reformation, many modern-day churches and denominations are teaching false doctrines. The devil, whose goal is to prevent people from knowing and understanding the truth of Jesus Christ, has twisted Scripture and deceived God's people. Truth has been suppressed, and as a result, people are not able to discern the signs of the times.

There seem to be four philosophies or views occurring in the church today. I realize these are broad generalities, but it is my purpose to help us understand the general state of the church today.

It seems that some churches are so scared of the world and culture that they've become fundamentalists and have withdrawn from engaging the world. They do not want to change the worship style or other aspects of the service. Some pastors are not preaching the true gospel of Jesus Christ, the gospel of grace! When people come to Christ, it is often out of fear of going to hell instead of a desire to be embraced by God's love and compassion. Yes, hell is real and it needs to be taught. But what is the motive of the gospel: fear or love? In some of these churches, laws and regulations are placed on new believers instead of the freedom that Jesus Christ gives us to live life abundantly. In many of these churches, they preach the gospel, and I believe that they hold to the Big 5 for the most part, but they're not being effective in reaching the lost and engaging the culture.

The second philosophy some churches have adopted is trying to make church worship services relevant and cultural, which I believe is appropriate. However, when it is the sole focus, worship services seem to become more of a concert with a light show instead of authentic worship. Many of the messages have been watered down and focus on what I call *pop theology*, which is a feel-good message with some Scripture added here and there, but little theological or biblical substance. Although this seems to be engaging the culture to some degree and seems to be reaching more people, there is shallowness in the message. The question about this ministry philosophy is, are they denying the power of teaching the Big 5 out of fear of being culturally irrelevant?

The third philosophy is even more damaging than the other two, because these churches as well as entire denominations are adopting the current culture and unbiblical practices of the world. Truth is watered down so as to not offend. There is a denying of some, if not all, of the Big 5, which they believe hinder or limit people from experiencing "love." This is one of the ultimate deceptive plans of the devil. When a church denies the foundational doctrines of the Christian Faith, then it ultimately denies the Christian Faith. When any pastor or church waters down the truth, they deny the transforming power of the gospel. The transformational, atoning work of Jesus Christ on the cross is denied! The church is being deceived, and some people don't even know it.

There is a fourth philosophy that many churches and pastors are following, and that is boldly holding to the Big 5. They not only stand on the Word of God, they are trying to be relevant to society, without compromising the Truth. Worship is relevant, meaningful, and authentic, drawing people into the presence of God, but it's not a concert. Their focus is on reaching the lost and making authentic disciples of Jesus who not only know the Word and sound theology, but are living it out incarnationally, meaning letting Jesus' life live through our daily lives.

This is the church I and many other pastors are trying to build. However, the temptations and challenges that compromise the current "post-Christian" culture in the Western world are strong. But we must stand firm and hold to the Big 5 no matter what, as the final Big 5 states: *"Soli Deo Gloria,"* for the Glory of God alone!

How Are God-Fearing People Being Deceived?

There are two reasons people are unaware of the deception that has crept into the church. First, and most disturbingly, this deception has come from the pulpit. Some pastors have stopped teaching the Big 5 every Christian should know. Sermons are filled with pop psychology, which is more focused on making people feel good than on sharing the gospel and making disciples.

People are being deceived because the church is not teaching the authority of the Word of God. On top of that, people are not consistently reading the word on their own; thus, they don't know what it says.

Paul referred to this in his second letter to Timothy. He said a time would come when people would gather around a great number of teachers who would tell them "what their itching ears want to hear" (2 Timothy 4:3 NIV). Leaders are afraid of offending people with the truth, instead of being bold enough to speak the truth in love.

The second reason people are being deceived is because the church is not teaching the authority of the Word of God. On top of that, people are not consistently reading the word on their own, thus, they don't know what it says.

Paul acknowledged the Berean Jews in the Book of Acts, telling them that they possessed nobler character than the Thessalonians because they "examined the Scriptures every day to see if what Paul said was true" (Acts 17:11 NIV). Today it seems that some people believe whatever their pastor says, rather than testing it against God's Word.

The goal of faith is to do the work of God in love. This kind of love comes from a pure heart, motivated by Christ in us.

A New Reformation

Today there is a need for a new reformation. In 1 Timothy 1:3 (NIV) we read, "As I urged you when I went to Macedonia, stay there in Ephesus so that you may command a certain man not to teach false doctrines any longer."

Paul challenged the leaders in the church of Ephesus to stop teaching false doctrine, myths, and endless genealogies. He wrote that these promoted controversies rather than God's Work (1 Timothy 1:3-4).

Paul taught that God's Work is always by faith. Faith is a foundational part of the Big 5. The goal of faith is to do the work of God in love. This kind of love comes from a pure heart, motivated by Christ in us (1 Timothy 1:5).

Paul continued, "We know that the law is good if one uses it properly. We also know that the law is made not for the righteous but for lawbreakers and rebels, the ungodly and sinful, the unholy and irreligious, for those who kill their fathers or mothers, for murderers..." (1 Timothy 1:8-9 NIV).

People are saved by grace through faith alone in Jesus Christ, who died on the cross for the sins of humankind.

In today's society, some would label Paul as being politically incorrect. However, God is not interested in being politically correct. He is concerned with sound doctrine and transforming people through His Son. Without a firm foundation in sound doctrine, God's people will be tossed to and fro with every wind and wave of doctrine. If people don't know the Big 5, they will begin to hold on to ideas and activities that sound or feel good.

Mainline churches—including the Presbyterian Church USA, the United Methodist, the United Church of Christ, the Episcopal Church in America, and others—have moved away from the foundations of the

Faith in significant ways. It is time for a new reformation.

People are saved by grace through faith alone in Jesus Christ, who died on the cross for the sins of humankind. Because of His death and resurrection, people can once again experience eternal life, here and now and for eternity. That's the gospel. No more, no less. Anything beyond that is a doctrine of demons when it comes to salvation.

Understanding the Big 5 will help believers grow their faith for the purpose of knowing and discerning truth from error. They are then free to do the work of God in love, as well as strengthen other believers in their faith.

WORKBOOK

Chapter One Questions

Question: After reading about the Big 5 of our faith, in what ways are you more aware of the modern church drifting away from the true teachings of the Bible? How does this awareness change your perception of what it means to follow Christ?

_____

_____

_____

_____

_____

_____

_____

_____

_____

_____

_____

Question: If the church forgets the Big 5, it will begin to lose direction, hope, foundation, and ultimately its impact on the world. In what ways have you observed this statement to be true? How can you strengthen your personal foundation of faith?

_____
_____
_____
_____
_____
_____
_____
_____
_____
_____

Question: The devil continues to deceive people by causing the church to be influenced by culture. What areas can you identify in which the culture has overrun the church? What is God calling on you to do to make a stand for the Word of God?

_____
_____
_____
_____
_____
_____
_____
_____
_____
_____

Question: Can you describe a time when you personally heard false teaching from a pastor or speaker? How did you respond? What steps can you take to be prepared for false teachers?

_____

_____

_____

_____

_____

_____

_____

_____

Action: During the Reformation, the Big 5 were developed and clarified because the Roman Catholic Church had been moving away from faithfully preaching and teaching the Word of God. If the church forgets the Big 5, it will begin to lose direction, hope, foundation, and ultimately its impact on the world. Just like the first-century church, the modern-day church in America and Europe is teaching false doctrine. Pastors are not preaching the true gospel of Jesus Christ. The devil continues to deceive people by causing the church to be influenced by culture. Without a firm foundation in sound doctrine, God's people will be tossed to and fro with every wind and wave of doctrine. If people don't know the Big 5 of our faith, they will begin to hold on to ideas and activities that sound or feel good instead of the truth. It is imperative we return to our foundations of faith. We can begin by studying God's Word and spending time in prayer. As with Martin Luther, change can begin with one person.

Chapter One Notes

CHAPTER TWO

What's the Word?

All Scripture is inspired by God and profitable for teaching, for reproof, for correction, for training in righteousness; so that the man of God may be adequate, equipped for every good work. — *2 Timothy 3:16-17 (NASB)*

The first of the Big 5 is known as *sola scriptura,* (Scripture alone), and it is the most important. Without grasping this doctrine, the church risks losing its solid foundation of faith, because people begin to look for other paths to God. They undermine the person and work of Jesus Christ, especially His atonement on the cross. They try to find other ways to obtain salvation and justification. They seek ways to justify their personal lifestyles and try to find other standards for so-called "moral living." Culture, more than Scripture, begins to shape the modern church, negatively influencing doctrine and practice.

Sola Scriptura

The doctrine of *sola scriptura* was foundational for leaders during the Reformation. This doctrine maintains that the Bible alone is the ultimate authority. This was the foundational principle of the Reformation. "Scripture alone is the sole infallible rule of faith for the church."[3] In other words Scripture alone is the rule of faith—that which governs and guides what Christians believe and why they believe it.[4]

As people heard the Word of God, they began to realize they didn't need to perform the required rituals and endless, rote prayers to the saints to obtain salvation.

The Reformation occurred in the 1500s. The Lord had chosen many men and women of God to stand against the corrupt Roman Catholic Church at the time. The Church had moved far away from faithfully preaching the Word. It had imposed rituals and rules that hindered common folks from growing closer to Christ.

Reformers urged the church to return to the purity of the Word of God. They saw the Word of God as the ultimate authority. Martin Luther, John Calvin, Huldrych Zwingli, and many others fought to reclaim the foundations of the faith.

As people heard the Word of God, they began to realize they didn't need to perform the required rituals and endless, rote prayers to the saints to obtain salvation. They realized they had the living Word dwelling in them, and this resulted in freedom.

Reformation had begun.

Luther and the other reformers realized that only the Scriptures teach how to love as Jesus loves. The church, ultimately, has no authority.

It was during this period that the Big 5 doctrines of our faith were clarified. These weren't new doctrines; they were merely being reestablished. But at the time, the Roman Catholic Church held immense power, and they came against those trying to reform the church.

Nevertheless, *sola scriptura* quickly took root. The Roman Catholic authorities interrogated Martin Luther at the Diet of Worms, a council held by the Holy Roman Emperor, in 1521. He was arrested, called a heretic, and put on trial for his teachings of Scripture alone and of salvation of grace by faith alone. At his interrogation, Martin Luther declared his conscience to be captive to the Word of God, saying:

I cannot submit my faith either to the pope or to the councils, because it is clear as the day that they have frequently erred and contradicted each other. Unless I am convinced by the testimonies from Scripture, or by the clearest reasoning—unless I am persuaded by means of the passages I have quoted—and unless they thus render my conscience bound by the Word of God, I cannot and I will not retract, for it is unsafe for a Christian to speak against his conscience. [Then Luther looked around at the assembly and spoke these famous words] Here I stand, I can do no other; May God help me! Amen![5]

What a powerful statement! Luther and the other reformers realized that only the Scriptures teach how to love as Jesus loves. The church, ultimately, has no authority.

Today there is indeed a need for a new reformation.

One of the great founders of our nation was President Thomas Jefferson. He was a brilliant man—an intellectual. God used him in amazing ways, but his view of the Scripture was skewed. He literally cut out every Scripture that described when Jesus or the apostles performed a miracle. What was left was Thomas Jefferson's own version of the Bible.

Jefferson believed Jesus was a godly, righteous man, but he didn't believe in miracles. Therefore, Jefferson decided he was not going to believe in particular passages of the Word of God. What pride! His view, not God's, was authoritative. But many people in the present day do this as well: They pick and choose what they like or don't like from God's Word.

Today there is indeed a need for a new reformation. Churches in many mainline denominations believe their decisions and standards for living are authoritative, even over Scripture.

The church and Christians must depend on Scripture alone to challenge such false teachings. James White summarizes this well, stating:

> Scripture alone is the inerrant rule of the church's life, but the evangelical church today has separated Scripture from its authoritative function. In practice, the church is guided, far too often, by the culture. Therapeutic technique, marketing strategies, and the beat of the entertainment world often have far more to say about what the church wants, how it functions and what it offers, than does the Word of God.[6]

The Bible Is the Word of God

When Jesus was being tempted by the devil, Satan promised Jesus the whole world if only He would bow down and worship him. "'All this I will give you,' Satan said, 'if you will bow down and worship me'" (Matthew 4:9 NIV).

If Jesus used the Word of God to teach who He is, then Christians need to take the Word seriously.

How did Jesus respond? He answered Satan with Scripture: "It is written: 'Worship the Lord your God, and serve him only'" (Matthew 4:10 NIV). If Jesus used the Word of God to teach who He is, then Christians need to take the Word seriously.

Now, please note that the Word of God is to be exalted, not worshipped. Only Jesus is to be worshipped, because He is the ultimate author of the Holy Scriptures. Yet all Scripture—not just some—is "God-breathed and is useful for teaching, rebuking, correcting and training in righteousness, so that the servant of God may be thoroughly equipped for every good work" (2 Timothy 3:16-17 NIV).

The words in Greek for God-breathed are *theopneustos,* which means, "breathed out by God." The New Testament theologian B. B. Warfield said that God-breathed "does not express a breathing *into* the Scriptures by God...What it affirms is that the Scriptures owe their origin to an activity of God, the Holy Spirit and are in the highest and truest sense, His creation. It is on this foundation the divine origin that all the high attributes of Scripture are built."[7]

The Westminster Confession of Faith, written in 1646, summarizes what Christians believe and emphasizes the doctrine of sola scriptura, saying "The Bible speaks authoritatively and so deserves to be believed and obeyed. This authority does not depend on the testimony of any man or church but completely on God, its author, who is himself truth. The Bible therefore is to be accepted as true, because it is the word of God."[8]

...nor ought we to consider custom, or the great multitude, or antiquity, or succession of times and persons, or councils, decrees or statutes, as of equal value with the truth of God...

Likewise, the Belgic Confession, written in 1561 during the Reformation, states: "We confess that this Word of God was not sent, nor delivered by the will of men, but that holy men of God spoke being moved by the Holy Spirit, as Peter says. [2 Peter 1:21] Afterwards our God, because of a special care he has for us and our salvation, commanded his servants, the prophets, and apostles, to commit his revealed Word to writing. He himself wrote with his own finger the two tables of the law. Therefore we call such writings holy and divine Scriptures" (Article 3).[9]

Article 7 of this Confession continues:

We believe that those Holy Scriptures fully contain the will of God, and that whatsoever man ought to believe, unto salvation, is sufficiently taught therein. For, since the whole manner of worship, which God requires of us, is written in them at large, it is unlawful for any one, though an apostle, to teach otherwise than we are now taught in the Holy Scriptures: nay, though it were an angel from heaven, as the apostle Paul saith.

For, since it is forbidden, to add unto or take away anything from the word of God, it doth thereby evidently appear, that the doctrine thereof is most perfect and complete in all respects. Neither do we consider of equal value any writing of men, however holy these men may have been, with those divine

Scriptures, nor ought we to consider custom, or the great multitude, or antiquity, or succession of times and persons, or councils, decrees or statutes, as of equal value with the truth of God, for the truth is above all; for all men are of themselves liars, and more vain than vanity itself. Therefore, we reject with all our hearts, whatsoever doth not agree with this infallible rule, which the apostles have taught us, saying, Try the spirits whether they are of God. Likewise, if there come any unto you, and bring not this doctrine, receive him not into your house.[10]

These are dynamic statements which are a part of the Protestant church's teachings. Yet today, many Christians seem to deny them and challenge the Word.

We must examine ourselves and ask the question: Do we believe the Bible to be the Word of God or not? Do we believe it to be the truth?

Moving Forward

There is much to learn from the reformers regarding sola scriptura. We must examine ourselves and ask the question: Do we believe the Bible to be the Word of God or not? Do we believe it to be the truth?

Josh McDowell has written extensively about understanding the inspiration for and authority of the Bible. The following is a summary of four different views of the Bible's inspiration from McDowell that will help us understand how easy it is for anyone to adopt a false view over the proper view.[11]

1. The Bible is an inspirational book, but it is no different from any other great literary work of the past. This view places Scripture on the same level as other human productions. It denies the possibility of God revealing Himself in the books of the Bible, and thus, it is a false belief. However, this theory is taught in some churches today. This view is simply not what Paul or Peter taught, and it's certainly not what Jesus believed.

The Bible is a book that is both divine and human.

2. The Bible is in part, and only in part, the Word of God. This view limits the manner and quantity in which a revelation of God can be contained in the books of the Bible. Proponents of this view say the Bible contains the Word of God or the Bible becomes the Word of God, but is not actually the Word of God. This is the position of some churches today, which gives the leadership ultimate authority on what is the Word of God and what is not, although it is all in the Bible.

3. The Bible is the divine Word of God, dictated by God to select human authors. This view leaves no room for the diversity in background and personality of the various individual writers. Some fundamentalists may hold to this view, although it is limiting. And as Dr. James I. Packer notes, "This 'dictation theory' is a man of straw." People are not robots. God selected men by

His Holy Spirit; He anointed them and inspired them by His Spirit to write His Word using their own personalities.

4. The Bible is a book that is both divine and human. This view reflects the biblical teaching that the Bible itself—in all that it states—is a production of divine revelation, channeled through, but uncorrupted by, human intervention. Each author's unique talents, backgrounds, and perspectives complement, rather than restrict, what God intended to reveal.

This view circles back to Paul's claim: "All Scripture is God-breathed and is useful for teaching, rebuking, correcting and training in righteousness, so that the man [or woman] of God may be thoroughly equipped for every good work" (2 Timothy 3:16-17 NIV).

If God inspired the writers of the Bible, then there must be authority in it for us to learn from and follow.

Sola scriptura—the authority of the Word of God in the life of the believer. The question is: Do *you* believe it?

Chapter Two Questions

Question: The church must depend on Scripture alone to challenge false teachings. We must examine ourselves and ask the question: Do you believe the Word of God to be the Word of God or not? Do you believe it to be the truth? In what ways has your walk with God or your worship become routine, or a matter of endless rituals? Is it because of what the church teaches?

_____

_____

_____

_____

_____

_____

_____

_____

_____

Question: All Scripture—not just some—is God-breathed and is useful for teaching, rebuking, correcting, and training in righteousness. In what ways have you picked and chosen what you like or don't like from God's Word? What is God revealing to you about the Scriptures you dislike?

_____

_____

_____

_____

_____

_____

_____

_____

_____

_____

Question: After reading the four views on the Bible's inspiration, how did your interpretation change? In the past or present, have you believed one or more of these views to be true? How is God showing you the truth of His Word?

_____

_____

_____

_____

_____

Question: How will you step out in faith to practice sola scriptura? What changes do you need to make to live fully, knowing that the Bible is the final authority?

_____

_____

_____

_____

_____

_____

_____

_____

Action: Scripture alone is the rule of faith—that which governs and guides what Christians believe and why they believe it. Only the Scriptures teach how to love as Jesus loves. Since Jesus used the Word of God to teach who He is, Christians need to take it seriously. If this has been a struggle for you, then ask God to help you recognize the truth of His word.

Chapter Two Notes

CHAPTER THREE

Keys to Interpreting Scripture

All Scripture is inspired by God and profitable for teaching, for reproof, for correction, for training in righteousness; so that the man of God may be adequate, equipped for every good work. — 2 Timothy 3:16-17 (NASB)

The Bible is a thick book, and to begin reading it from Genesis can be daunting! If you add in a few Hebrew names and genealogies, many people quickly lose interest or become overwhelmed. Perhaps you may feel uneducated as you try to understand certain passages. This magnificent book, containing sixty-six books, written by at least thirty-nine different authors, spanning different genres of literature for over approximately 1,500 years, can sometimes be intimidating to read. Sometimes it can seem impossible to understand, not to mention properly interpreted. However, the Bible is a book that can be interpreted accurately with some basic principles and strategies that everyone can learn to use.

Key Principles to Interpreting Scripture

There have been times when I've been sharing a passage from the Bible and someone has commented, "Well, that's your interpretation, and the Bible can be interpreted any way you want." I believe it is most likely that they were being convicted by the Word of God and didn't like what the Holy Spirit was saying.

There are universal principles to the Bible. If those basic principles are used, then anyone who studies Scripture can interpret the Bible as accurately as possible.

Over the years, I've crafted my response to such comments. I will say, "That is my interpretation, but there are universal principles to interpreting the Bible. If those basic principles are used, then anyone who studies Scripture can interpret the Bible as accurately as possible."

Instead of two people coming up with completely opposite interpretations, these basic principles knit different interpretations together with an element of the same truth. The results are two interpretations that are very close and give a fuller understanding to the passage, but not two completely different and opposite interpretations.

Not only can the Bible be deliberately manipulated to justify one's position, but the many tools available for studying the Bible can be abused as well. Some people approach Scripture with emotional baggage: Everyone has a different background and a variety of life experiences. Some look for passages in Scripture to prove their own personal experience.

The challenge is to approach Scripture with a mind ready to be taught by the Holy Spirit. Personal issues need to be left behind. Following these principles will guard against misusing even a single word in Scripture for personal agendas.

Let's learn once again from the apostle Paul. As 2 Timothy 2:15 recounts, Paul was sitting in a Roman prison and sensed his time on earth might be coming to an end. Paul had pastored the church in Ephesus for three years and poured his heart into the people of Ephesus. Timothy had heard Paul's teaching and had ministered alongside him many times.

Do your best to present yourself to God as one approved, a worker who does not need to be ashamed and who correctly handles the word of truth (2 Timothy 2:15 NIV).

Paul had commissioned Timothy to continue pastoring the young Ephesian church. Timothy was young and some of the church elders were looking down on him. To complicate things, false teachings had crept in.

And so Paul instructed Timothy, "Do your best to present yourself to God as one approved, a worker who does not need to be ashamed and who correctly handles the word of truth" (2 Timothy 2:15 NIV).

Paul encouraged Timothy to be an evangelist, a teacher, and a pastor. He exhorted the younger man to continue to work in Ephesus and to do so with his whole heart. Timothy was to be "a workman who is not ashamed of his calling, and who correctly handles the word of truth."

The New Testament was not complete at this time, but the Gospel of Mark had already been penned. In all likelihood, the apostles had started to pass around the Gospel of Mark to the churches. Paul was exhorting Timothy to correctly handle the Old Testament, as well as this first gospel.

The question is this: How can Christians avoid misinterpreting the Word of God? Here are three methods.

1. How to Approach the Bible

Do we view this big book with fear, in the sense that we say to ourselves, "there is no way I can ever read, much less understand the Bible"? Or do we view the Bible as just one of many inspired and spiritual book?

John Calvin, a theologian during the Reformation in the 1500s, has a great statement about the view of the Bible. He wrote:

Now this power [of inspiration] which is peculiar to Scripture is clear from the fact that of human writings, however artfully polished, there is none capable of affecting us at all comparably. Read Demosthenes or Cicero; read Plato, Aristotle, and others of that tribe. They will, I admit, allure you, delight you, move you, enrapture you in wonderful measure. But betake yourself from them to this sacred reading. Then, in spite of yourself, so deeply will it affect you, so penetrate your heart, so fix itself in your very marrow, that, compared with its deep impression, such vigor as the orators and philosophers have will nearly vanish. Consequently, it is easy to see that the Scriptures, which so far surpass all gifts and graces of human endeavor, breathe something divine.[12]

This statement is very accurate. So how do we approach the Scripture? What is our attitude of the Bible?

The way we view the Bible, as well as our approach or attitude towards it, truly affects how we will study it and whether we will study it properly. Our view of the Word is vital to receive what God desires to impart into our lives through it.

- Some approach the Word to discover special, hidden meanings, which usually "spiritualizes" the Word. This can be very dangerous.
- Others approach it mainly from an End-Times perspective, which limits their interpretations.
- Some just believe there are several different ways to interpret the Bible and therefore everyone's interpretation is correct. This is what I believe the majority of people think, because there has been

very little taught on proper methods and principles of studying the Bible.

- Some people begin reading it with fear.
- Some rely on others to interpret it for them.
- Some view it as equal to many other spiritual books on the market.
- Others don't believe the Bible is the Holy Word of God, but some interesting literature, poetry, history, fables, etc.

The last two views are what one famous celebrity believes: Bill Maher, Jr. Mr. Maher is an American comedian, writer, producer, political commentator, actor, media critic, and television host. He also is an atheist.

He invited one of my friends, Dr. Ralph Reed, to be a guest on his show to promote his book *Awakening*.[13] Mr. Maher asked my friend, "Do you really believe that the Word of God is the Holy Scriptures?" and Ralph answered, "Yeah, I really do."

The way we view the Bible, as well as our approach or attitude towards it, truly affects how we will study it and whether we will study it properly.

Maher then said, "How can you believe in a so-called God who says you're supposed to kill everybody? And what about when God says if you catch an adulterous woman in the act, you are to stone her to death? That's not a loving God." Maher was throwing sarcastic comments out left and right, and Ralph handled each question beautifully.

One thing Ralph said was, "First of all, you are picking and choosing verses and not looking at the context of the passage." Maher couldn't respond, and the way Ralph stayed calm and answered every question to the best of his ability frustrated the host all the more.

The point to the original question of how we approach the Bible is foundational, and also the first step to proper interpretation. How do *you* view the Bible and approach it?

2. A Well-Prepared Mind

A mind that is thinking of a million different things won't be well prepared to hear from God and interpret Scripture. We all live busy lives with numerous responsibilities. There is always something looming before us that needs to be done, or some activity we are anticipating. Most of us spend precious few minutes of our day on the Word. Ask God to clear your mind and help you focus as you read His Word.

A mind that is thinking of a million different things won't be well prepared to hear from God and interpret Scripture.

3. A Well-Prepared Heart

Because I am committed to reading the Word every day, I will sometimes grab my Bible, read a passage, and check off that I read it for that day. However, this does not necessarily mean my heart was ready to receive from God.

One's attitude and approach to the Word of God make all the difference in receiving a word from God. Almost every morning, right before I open my Bible, I pray: "Lord, I commit this day to You. I set aside my cares and thoughts of what I have to do today. I ask You to cover my mind with Your precious blood. I bind the enemy and any confusion that would try to come to me. Lord, prepare me to receive a word from You today."

This simple prayer prepares my heart to receive a word from God through His holy Word, the Bible.

Three Keys for Bible Study

How then do we "correctly handle the Word of Truth" as Paul commanded Timothy? There are three major keys for proper interpretation in studying the Bible: Observation, Interpretation, and Application.[14] This is known as the Inductive Bible Study Method, and I believe it is the best method for studying the Bible.

This is because it helps us ask the right questions. The Bible in proper context and context of the passage is foundational. As Kay Arthur states, "context always rules in interpretation."[15] There a famous statement about this that goes: "The text taken out of context becomes a pretext," which will always lead to a misinterpretation. As Gordon Fee states, "A text cannot mean what it never meant."[16]

Let's briefly look at these three key principles.

1. Observation

The first principle of studying the Bible is observation. Observing the text means asking the question: "What does the passage say?" If this step is skipped, the following two steps will be ineffective. People are too quick to jump right to interpretation or application. Pause and ask some key observational questions. What does the passage say?

Paul had written to Timothy to encourage him to stand firm on the truth and also to bring correction where correction was needed.

Earlier I offered observation about the passage in 2 Timothy. Timothy was the new pastor of Ephesus. There were some false teachers who had entered into the church. Paul had written to Timothy to encourage him to stand firm on the truth and also to bring correction where correction was needed.

Paul then said, "Avoid godless chatter because those who indulge in it will become more and more ungodly" (2 Timothy 2:16 NIV). Now, here is the observation: In verse 15, Timothy was exhorted to handle the word of truth correctly because there were godless people in his church who spat godless chatter. What godless chatter was Paul talking about? Do an observation! Go back and read the previous verse or verses to help you understand the whole picture.

Understanding both the literal and historical context is also important when interpreting the Word.

At the time Paul wrote this letter to Timothy, the false teaching of Gnosticism had entered into the church. Gnosticism comes from the Greek word *gnosis*, meaning "knowledge." A simple understanding of Gnosticism is that it spiritualizes everything; it taught that a special knowledge could be reached by giving up material possessions. Thus, the Gnostics considered the material world to be evil.

In 2 Timothy 2: 17-18, Paul referred to two men who were false teachers within the church, comparing their teaching to spreading gangrene. The false teaching was that the resurrection had already occurred and that it was a spiritual resurrection, not a physical one. This teaching was likely a form of Gnosticism.

This is what it looks like to form observations of Scripture. It takes a little time, but it is important in order to handle the word of truth correctly. In this case, Paul's original intent was to build up Timothy—to encourage him to be a great pastor and a great teacher of the Word.

Understanding both the literal and historical context is also important when interpreting the Word. What kind of literature is it? Is it poetry? Is it a parable? Is it allegorical? Is it historical? Never take Scripture out of context. The context for the passage from 2 Timothy chapter 2 is avoiding godless chatter because false doctrines were spreading.

Allow the Scripture to interpret Scripture. For example, in Colossians 2, Paul wrote: "See to it that no one takes you captive through hollow and deceptive philosophy which depends on human tradition and the elemental spiritual forces of this world rather than Christ" (Colossians 2:8 NIV). If you apply the teaching here to the passage in 2 Timothy 2, then you have a more complete observation and understanding.

Read with purpose. Ask who, what, when, where, why, and how. To whom was the author writing this? Who was the audience? Who was the author? What was going on? How did the audience receive the Word?

Finally, read with purpose. Ask who, what, when, where, why, and how. To whom was the author writing this? Who was the audience? Who was the author? What was going on? How did the audience receive the Word? Why was there such tension between the Pharisees and Jesus all the time?

This may sound like an English class when the teacher taught you how to read with purpose by asking the five W's and H: Who, What, Where, When, Why, and How. It's the same when studying the Bible. Observation is foundational to interpretation and application.

Jumping ahead to 2 Timothy 3:16-17, Paul explains that "Scripture is God-breathed and is useful for teaching, rebuking, correcting, training and righteousness so that the servant of God may be thoroughly equipped for every good work" (NIV). As you observe, I encourage writing in your Bible. For example, circle the connecting phrase "so that" and say "Purpose." Such phrases as "so that" and "in order that" indicate that a purposeful statement is coming. The purpose of the Bible is not only for teaching, rebuking, and correcting in righteousness, but "so that the servant of God may be thoroughly equipped for every good work."

Paul was teaching Timothy how to handle the word of truth, both to be able to teach others sound doctrine, and to rebuke others within the body of Christ. This was done in order to bring correction, so people would repent from their sins. Just like parents discipline their children in order to keep them on the right path, God encourages correction within the body of Christ.

This is only a summary of what observation is all about. For further study in greater detail, purchase Kay Arthur's *How to Study Your Bible,* and Gordon Fee and Douglas Stuart's *How to Read the Bible for All Its*

Worth. These two books alone will help you become a solid reader and interpreter of the Bible.

Always seek the full counsel of the Word of God when interpreting. This means searching out other places in Scripture that give support or clarity to the passage being interpreted.

2. Interpretation

Observation is followed by interpretation, also called *exegesis.* Exegesis is the careful and systematic study of Scripture to discover the author's original intent. It is basically an attempt to hear the Word as the original recipient heard it.[17]

A text cannot mean what it was never intended to mean. This happens when Scripture is taken out of context. For example, Jesus said, "If your hand causes you to sin, cut it off" (Matthew 5:30). Jesus was talking in hyperbole, using exaggeration to make a point.

When interpreting, it also is important to understand the culture in which the text was written. This was typically the first-century Middle East. Many take their current life and try to interpret Scripture from their own perspective, rather than within the cultural and historical context in which it was written. This causes problems in interpretation. I believe one of the biggest problems today, for the church and for individuals, is reading and interpreting the Scripture through current times and standards while transferring our beliefs onto the passage. This is incorrect! We must try, to the best of our ability, to allow the context of the passage to mean what it means without putting our twenty-first-century view onto it.

Always seek the full counsel of the Word of God when interpreting. This means searching out other places in Scripture that give support or clarity to the passage being interpreted. For example, there are many passages in the Bible that speak about men and women in ministry. One such passage specifically mentions that women should not teach men. Yet a study of the full counsel of God reveals there were women teachers in the Bible.

> *Always interpret the Old Testament in light of the information in the New Testament.*

Furthermore, always interpret the Old Testament in light of the information in the New Testament. Many Bibles today cross-reference verses in the margins so you can further study other related areas of Scripture. Often Bibles also include a brief subject index or concordance in the back.

As mentioned above, this is only a simple summary of how to interpret the Bible. For learning more principles, use the books by Gordon Fee and Douglas Stuart as well as Kay Arthur.

3. Application

After observing and interpreting the text, ask the question: "What does this mean to me today?" Or ask, "What does this mean for the church today?" Consider how to apply biblical principles to your everyday life.

It is important to remember that we need to allow the Word of God to change us, without us trying to change the Word to fit our beliefs, lifestyles, or practices. We need to learn to submit our emotions, our feelings, and our culture to the Word and not the other way around.

God wants to speak to us through His Word. He wants to reveal Himself and the truth to us through His Word. He desires to transform us by the Holy Spirit, who anointed men of God to give us the Holy Bible. So, approach the Bible with these principles and be prepared to be changed.

Sola scriptura, Scripture alone, is the first of the Big 5. As we learn to confirm our life and our beliefs with the Scripture, we will be renewed and transformed. From this first Big 5, all the others are discovered, but without the second Big 5, the others can't stand.

WORKBOOK

Chapter Three Questions

Question: What study tools or methods have you used in the past or present to study Scripture? How have they helped you discover more about the Word of God? Which tools would you recommend to others?

_____

_____

_____

_____

_____

_____

_____

_____

_____

_____

Question: How do you prepare yourself to read or study the Bible? Is this easy for you? Why or why not?

_____
_____
_____
_____
_____
_____
_____
_____
_____
_____
_____

Question: Why do you think God desires for us to read His Word daily? How has God spoken to you through His Word?

_____
_____
_____
_____
_____
_____
_____
_____
_____

Question: When you read a verse or passage, go back and read the previous verse or verses to help you understand the whole picture. Is this a new concept for you? If so, how can you implement this in your study? If you are already practicing this technique, how have you benefited from it?

_____

_____

_____

_____

_____

_____

_____

_____

_____

_____

Question: How could a careful and systematic study of Scripture benefit your personal study of the Word of God? In what new ways will you search out Scripture? How will you apply the things you learn to your life?

_____

_____

_____

_____

_____

_____

_____

_____

_____

_____

Action: The Bible is a large book, and it can seem overwhelming when we start to read it! If you add in a few Hebrew names and genealogies, many people quickly lose interest or become overwhelmed. Sometimes it can seem impossible to understand, not to mention interpret properly. Too often the Bible or the many tools available for studying the Bible are deliberately manipulated to justify one's position or sin. Everyone has a different background, with a variety of life experiences. Your attitude and approach to the Word of God make all the difference in receiving a word from Him. Ask God to show you what He has for you in the passage you are reading or studying.

Then the first key to studying the Bible is observing the text and asking the question: What does the passage say? When you read a verse or passage, go back and read the previous verse or verses to help you understand the whole picture. Observation is followed by interpretation, or exegesis: a careful and systematic study of Scripture to discover the author's original intent.

God gave us the Bible so we could learn more about Him—so don't be shy in using it!

Chapter Three Notes

CHAPTER FOUR

Christ Alone

Jesus answered, "I am the way and the truth and the life. No one comes to the Father except through me." — John 14:6 (NIV)

Is Jesus really the only way to salvation, eternal life, and true inner peace? Aren't there many ways to God? Why does Jesus say He is the only way to eternal life? Isn't that being exclusive? These are major questions many nonbelievers ask, but they are also questions Christians ask. These are all legitimate; so what are the answers?

One of the best ways to answer these questions and to begin to understand the second of the Big 5 is by reading the lyrics of a tremendous modern hymn written by Stuart Townend and Keith Getty, titled "In Christ Alone."

In Christ alone my hope is found,
He is my light, my strength, my song;

This Cornerstone, this solid Ground,
Firm through the fiercest drought and storm.
What heights of love, what depths of peace,
When fears are stilled, when strivings cease!
My Comforter, my All in All,
Here in the love of Christ I stand.

In Christ alone!—who took on flesh,
Fullness of God in helpless babe.
This gift of love and righteousness,
Scorned by the ones He came to save:
Till on that cross as Jesus died,
The wrath of God was satisfied—
For every sin on Him was laid;
Here in the death of Christ I live.

There in the ground His body lay,
Light of the world by darkness slain:
Then bursting forth in glorious day
Up from the grave He rose again!
And as He stands in victory
Sin's curse has lost its grip on me,
For I am His and He is mine—
Bought with the precious blood of Christ.

No guilt in life, no fear in death,
This is the power of Christ in me;
From life's first cry to final breath,
Jesus commands my destiny.
No power of hell, no scheme of man,
Can ever pluck me from His hand:
Till He returns or calls me home,
Here in the power of Christ I'll stand.[18]

This beautiful song expresses the truth that Jesus Christ is the only way to eternal life; the only way to a relationship with God, the Father and Creator of the universe; the only way to inner peace; the only way to real purpose in life. To understand the second *sola*,

Christ Alone or *solus Christus*, we need to go to the Scriptures and reveal why this statement is the truth. Then we can address the earlier questions.

Why is Jesus the only way?...Because that is the way God ordained it.

The statement that "Jesus is the only way to salvation or eternal life and true inner peace" sounds highly exclusive and seems to offend many people. Why is Jesus the only way? The simple and direct answer is because that is how God ordained it. Another answer is to say that we read it in the Scriptures—and as we have learned in the previous chapters, the Scripture is the true, inspired, and infallible Word of God. We read in the Gospel of John 14:6, where Jesus Christ Himself declares: "I am the way and the truth and the life. No one comes to the Father except through me." If this is correct, then don't we have to believe what Jesus said is true?

When people get upset with me because they hear me make this statement, I say to them, "Don't get mad at me—talk to Jesus about it. He is the one who said it."

But before we get too far into this topic, let's look at a few passages in Scripture that support Jesus's statement in John 14:6, as well as the overall context of these passages and their relevant theological concepts.

In John 3, Jesus is talking with Nicodemus, a Jewish spiritual leader and a member of the Sanhedrin, which was the governing body of the Jewish faith. In their conversation, Jesus states:

> No one has ascended into heaven, but He who descended from heaven: the Son of Man. As Moses lifted up the serpent in the wilderness, even so must the Son of Man be lifted up; so that whoever believes will in Him have eternal life.
>
> For God so loved the world, that He gave His only begotten Son, that whoever believes in Him shall not perish, but have eternal life. For God did not send the Son into the world to judge the world, but that the world might be saved through Him. He who believes in Him is not judged; he who does not believe has been judged already, because he has not believed in the name of the only begotten Son of God. — *John 3:13-18 (NASB)*

Jesus is talking about Himself and invoking the Old Testament prophets Moses and Isaiah, of whom Nicodemus would have been familiar. Then He says that the Savior must be lifted up in death, in the resurrection and in the exaltation, for people to be saved. (See Numbers 21:9-10 and Isaiah 52:13).

Jesus is emphasizing that having faith in Him is the only way to receive eternal life with God. Remember, this is Jesus speaking, not someone else. Now let's look at a few more passages in the Bible on this subject.

Peter, an Apostle of Jesus, had just been used by God to heal a lame man. For this act, and his preaching of the good news about Jesus Christ, he was brought before the Jewish leadership council to explain how this man was healed. So Peter tells them about Jesus—who He was and is, what He did, and how He was raised from the dead. Then Peter makes one of the most profound statements about *solus Christus*. He states: "And there is salvation in no one else [besides Jesus]; for there is no other name [besides Jesus] under heaven that has been given among men by which we must be saved" (Acts 4:12 NASB).

> *There wasn't a question in Peter's mind that there was any other way to eternal life besides Jesus.*

Peter does not say that one can be saved or find eternal life through works, through believing in Buddha or another person, or through another religious way or practice. He declares that Jesus Christ is the only way one can be saved and receive eternal life. There is no question in Peter's mind. Based on his understanding of Jesus and all that He taught him and the other disciples, there's no other way to eternal life. Peter was clear and direct.

Paul, another Apostle of Jesus, writes extensively about how one is saved and receives eternal life. In the Letter to the Romans, Paul makes a statement that is similar to Peter's about salvation. In the context of chapters 9 and 10, Paul reveals that the Messiah is not just for the Jews, but also for all people who believe. He writes that "if you confess with your mouth Jesus as Lord, and believe in your heart that God raised him from the dead, you will be saved … for 'WHOEVER WILL CALL ON THE NAME OF THE LORD [JESUS] WILL BE SAVED.'" (Romans 10:9, 13 NASB).

Paul, like Peter, does not give any other possibility of salvation and eternal life except through Jesus. We could spend hours studying the Bible, especially the New Testament, only to discover the exclusiveness of Jesus and what He does for all those who believe.

Throughout the Word of God, we see God setting the standards and practices for how to come to Him, have fellowship with Him, and salvation from Him.

Now, returning to the main statement of Jesus in John 14:6: "I am the way and the truth and the life. No one comes to the Father except through Me." How could Jesus and the others be so bold and direct about how one can know God and experience eternal life?

In the context of this passage in John 14, Jesus is just teaching His disciples about what is about to come in the next couple of hours, days, and weeks. It is the Jewish feast of Passover, and Jesus gathers His disciples to celebrate this occasion. However, He then begins to prepare them for His arrest, His trials, His brutal beatings and suffering, and then His crucifixion and resurrection, along with the promise of the Holy Spirit to empower them for ministry after He ascends to the Father.

This is overwhelming to the disciples! Think about it: The one you believe is the true Messiah, God in the flesh, whom all the Prophets and the Scriptures promised, is talking about dying a brutal death on a cross and going to the Father. Don't you think, if you were there hearing Jesus, you would be asking a lot of questions? Thus, the disciples ask Jesus to explain. In this context, Jesus makes the declaration that He is the only way to the Father and to eternal life (John 14:6).

Dr. Andreas Kostenberger offers excellent insight to Jesus's statement:

> Jesus as *the* one *way* to *the Father* fulfills the OT [Old Testament] symbols and teachings that show the exclusiveness of God's claim, such as the curtain (Ex. 26:33) barring access to God's presence from all except the Levitical high priest (Leviticus 16), the rejection of human inventions as means to approach God (Lev. 10:2), and the choice of Aaron alone to represent Israel before God in his sanctuary (Num. 17:5). Jesus is the only "way" to God (Acts 4:12), and he alone can provide access to God.[19]

Throughout the Word of God, we see God setting the standards and practices for how to come to Him, have fellowship with Him, and salvation from Him. This is manifested in the Son of God, Jesus Christ.

In Christ alone!

Who Is Jesus?

Why does Jesus make such dogmatic claims about Himself? How could He say He's "the only way," along with many similarly bold statements about Himself? For example, Jesus states: "Truly, truly, I say to you, before Abraham was born, I am" (John 8:58 NASB).

This statement alone is a declaration that Jesus Himself is God. How do we know that? Because in the context of the passage, the Jewish people are shocked that Jesus claims to be the great "I Am", meaning God, Himself. To them this is blasphemy; therefore they pick up rocks to stone Jesus to death.

If we do not believe who Jesus Christ is and what the Bible reveals about Him, then we are susceptible to deception.

In the Gospel of Mark, when Jesus is being tried before the Jewish high court for no other reason than being perceived as a threat to the Jewish leadership, the high priest asks Jesus, "'Are You the Christ, the Son of the Blessed One?' And Jesus said, 'I am; and you shall see THE SON OF MAN SITTING AT THE RIGHT HAND OF POWER, AND COMING WITH THE CLOUDS OF HEAVEN'" (Mark 14:61-62, NASB; see also Matthew 26:62-66). As in John 8:59, the leadership claims this to be blasphemy, for the high priest tears his clothes—one of their customs when someone blasphemes—and shouts, "You have heard the blasphemy" (Mark 14:64 NIV). The Jewish leadership knows that Jesus has just claimed to be God.

Jesus makes many other statements about Himself and who He is. Throughout the Bible, both in the Old Testament and the New Testament, we discover who Jesus Christ is and why He is God's plan for salvation, redemption, and eternal and abundant life.

So who is Jesus Christ really?

In Matthew 16:15-16, Jesus asks His disciples, "'But who do you say that I am?' Simon Peter answered, 'You are the Christ, the Son of the living God!'" (NASB). That is the question for us to ask today. Another theologian, Donald McLeod, asks this question in another way: "What makes Christ different?"[20] In other words, what makes Jesus Christ unique in terms of being the only way to salvation and having a personal relationship with God?

As we consider these questions, we can reflect on what the great reformer Martin Luther writes about Jesus Christ:

> The history of the Church Universal has confirmed in me the conviction that those who have had and maintained the central article in its integrity, that of Jesus Christ, have remained safely entrenched in their Christian faith...He who steadfastly holds to the doctrine that Jesus Christ is true God and true man, who died and rose again for us, will acquiesce in and heartily assent to all the other articles of the Christian faith.[21]

If we do not believe in who Jesus Christ is and what the Bible reveals about Him, then we are susceptible to deception, false teachings, and doctrines that lead us away from this central truth of "Christ alone" for salvation. This moves us away from the first of the Big 5 —Scripture alone—as our authority. Can we understand how important all these Big 5 are, and how they are all connected?

Once again, as we look at this second of the Big 5, we must rely on Scripture. Before we look further into who Jesus Christ is, I want to reemphasize the inspiration and importance of Scripture. Because if we do not believe the Bible is the inspired, infallible, and inerrant Word of God, then all the teachings and the life of Jesus are in doubt and may not be true.

> *Jesus was either a liar or a lunatic, or He was and is our Lord, the Son of God.*

With this foundation, let us continue to discover who Jesus Christ is. C. S. Lewis uses an argument known as the trilemma, in which Lewis emphasizes that Jesus was either a liar or a lunatic, or He was and is our Lord and Son of God. Let's briefly consider the trilemma.

We have already looked at just a few statements that Jesus made about who He was, equating Himself to be God. However, as John Davis writes in his book *Handbook of Basic Bible Texts*, "The deity of Jesus Christ in Scripture is demonstrated with reference to divine titles, divine attributes, divine actions, and New

Testament texts that specifically state an equality or identity between God and Christ."[22]

The following list about Jesus, described with divine titles and attributes, is derived from Davis. I hope you will take the time to study each passage about Jesus:[23]

Jesus is equated with the mighty God:

Isaiah 9:6; Isaiah 40:3; Malachi 3:1; 4:5; Joel 2:32; Mark 1:2–3; Luke 1:17; Acts 2:21

Jesus is the Son of God in a unique sense (the one and only begotten):

John 3:16-18; Matthew 26:63–65; Mark 14:60–64; Luke 22:67–70.

Jesus has divine attributes and qualities:

John 1:1-3, 29; 17:5; Philippians 2:5–7; Revelation 4:11; 5:9-14; 7:10–17; 19:1–9; 22:13.

Jesus is not limited by space:

Matthew 28:20; 18:20; Ephesians 1:22–23.

Jesus has universal power and authority:

Matthew 28:18; Philippians 2:9–11; Ephesians 1:22; John 3:35; 5:27; Colossians 1:16–17.

Jesus has life in Himself:

John 1:3–4; 5:26; 11:25; 14:6; Colossians 1:16; Hebrews 1:2.

Jesus sustains the universe:

Colossians 1:17.

Jesus has authority to forgive:

Mark 2:5–12; Matthew 9:2–6; Luke 5:20–24; 7:48.

Jesus is the object of prayer and worship:

Matthew 28:16–17; John 1:3; 14:13–14, 26; 15:16; 16:23-26; 20:28; Acts 7:59; Revelation 4:11; 5:9–14; 7:10–17; Philippians 2:5–11 (a hymn about Jesus).

Jesus has the power to raise the dead:

Matthew 9:23–25; Mark 5:35–43; Luke 7:22; 8:51–55; John 5:21; 11:25–26.

Jesus is the final judge of humankind:

Matthew 25:1–32; John 5:22, 27; Revelation 20:11–15; 22:12–16.

There is equality or identity in Jesus Christ and God:

John 1:1–4, 14; 8:48–59; 10:29–33; 14:6–9; 20:28; Philippians 2:5–11; Colossians 2:9; Titus 2:13; Hebrew 1:8; 2 Peter 1:1–2; Revelations 1:8, 17–18.

In light of all of these verses and titles regarding who Jesus is, in which many of them Jesus Himself is the speaker, it is difficult to deny who Jesus is.

Now that we have established from Scripture who Jesus says He is, reinforced with other verses in Scripture emphasizing that Jesus is God, let's address C. S. Lewis's trilemma: If Jesus is not who He says He is, nor does the Bible emphasize He is (the Second Person of the Holy Trinity), then He has to be either a liar or a lunatic.

Lewis begins his argument this way:

> Among these Jews there suddenly turns up a man who goes about talking as if He was God. He claims to forgive sins. He says He has always existed. He says He is coming to judge the world at the end of time...God, in their language, meant the Being outside the world, who had made it and was infinitely different from anything else. And when you have grasped that, you will see that what this man [Jesus] said was, quite simply, the most

shocking thing that has ever been uttered by human lips.[24]

He is putting into context how the Jewish people were dealing with the teachings, the miracles, and the claims of Jesus. Some did believe He was insane (see Mark 3:21 and John 10:20-21), yet how could someone who is insane do all that He did, living life in purity and holiness and teaching the Word of God the way He did?

If Jesus is not who He says He is, then He must be the greatest deceiver ever, having tricked people into believing in Him and following Him. Then His disciples continued His lies and deceived billions of people who believe Jesus is God and Savior. But again, the Bible is clear that Satan, not Jesus, is the father of lies and the great deceiver.

When we study the work and person of Jesus Christ...then we know He must be who He said He was and is.

Therefore, as Josh McDowell[25] clarifies Lewis's argument, if Jesus is not who He claimed to be, then there are only two choices:

1. Jesus knew His claims were false and continued to deceive through His teachings, His miracles, and His life. If this were the case, would He truly go through all the sufferings and the barbaric execution on the cross to secure His deception? I don't think so.

2. If Jesus really didn't know that His claims were false and truly believed His own claims about who He was, then He would have been a lunatic and deluded. Yet He still caused His disciples to believe in Him. Therefore, His disciples had to be lunatics because most of them were persecuted for their faith in Jesus.

C. S. Lewis summarizes this argument, stating:

> I am trying here to prevent anyone saying the really foolish thing that people often say about Him [Jesus]: "I'm ready to accept Jesus as a great moral teacher, but I don't accept His claim to be God." That is the one thing we must not say. A man who was merely a man and said the sort of things Jesus said would not be a great moral teacher. He would either be a lunatic—on a level with the man who says he is a poached egg—or else he would be the Devil of Hell. You must make your choice. Either this man was, and is, the Son of God: or else a madman or something worse. You can shut Him up for a fool, you can spit at Him and kill Him as a demon; or you can fall at His feet and call Him Lord and God. But let us not come with any patronizing nonsense about His being a great human teacher. He has not left that open to us. He did not intend to.[26]

When we study the person and work of Jesus Christ and understand who He claims to be, what He taught, what He did, what He said about Himself, and what the rest of the Bible reveals about Him, then we know He must be who He said He was and is. And when He states in John 14:6, "I am the way and the truth and the life. No one comes to the Father except through Me," then it is the truth, for Jesus cannot lie.

Therefore, the second of the Big 5 truly is foundational for us to believe: "Christ alone," *solus Christus*! It is only through Jesus's death on the cross for our sins, shame, guilt, and pain, and through His physical resurrection, that we are born again and given new life. Jesus alone is the way to salvation, eternal life, and the abundant life He came to give you and me.

Do you believe in Jesus Christ as your Lord and Savior?

WORKBOOK

Chapter Four Questions

Question: Who do you say that Jesus is? Why do you believe this?

_____

_____

_____

_____

_____

_____

_____

_____

_____

_____

Question: What do Jesus's claims about Himself reveal about His identity?

_____

_____

_____

_____

_____

_____

_____

_____

_____

_____

_____

Question: What do Jesus's actions reveal about his identity and God's relationship with us?

_____

_____

_____

_____

_____

_____

_____

_____

_____

_____

Question: What is your reaction to the statement "Jesus is the only way to salvation and eternal life?"

_____

_____

_____

_____

_____

_____

_____

_____

_____

_____

_____

Question: How do other people you know react to statements like "Jesus is the only way to salvation and eternal life"? How could you respond to someone who says this statement is exclusive?

_____

_____

_____

_____

_____

_____

_____

_____

_____

_____

_____

Action: Jesus was either a liar, a lunatic, or Lord—and His claim to lordship may be exclusive, but it's true. Scripture backs up the truth of His identity through its accounts of His teachings, claims, and actions. Jesus's death and resurrection are our only path to salvation and eternal life. Therefore, hold fast to the Word of God and don't be deceived by those who insist that there are many paths to God and life. Trust in Jesus alone for the forgiveness of your sins and to bring you inner peace.

Chapter Four Notes

CHAPTER FIVE

Grace Alone

For it is by grace you have been saved, through faith—
and this is not from yourselves, it is the gift of God...
— Ephesians 2:8 (NIV)

Have you ever wondered if there's more to life? This was the case with Nicodemus in the Bible. A Pharisee at the top of his field and a Sanhedrin member, Nicodemus approached Jesus at night, and according to John chapter 3, he asked: "We know, Jesus, that You are from God because of all the things You do, but how do we *really* know?"

Jesus knew that behind this question was a deeper longing: "How can I know God?"

Jesus told Nicodemus, "Unless one is born again he cannot see the kingdom of God" (John 3:3 NASB).

This leads us to the most humbling of the sola, the one that deals with the big question: How are people saved? This is what Nicodemus wanted to know.

It's a question that has been asked throughout the ages. During the Reformation, Martin Luther and other reformers grappled with this very question. At that time in the 1500s, it was taught that a person was saved by and through the Church. In addition, good works were required to be saved.

> *The church plays a role in proclaiming the good news, but salvation does not come through the church or its teachings. Good deeds will not accomplish a single thing toward one's salvation.*

As the reformers studied the Word of God, their hearts were drawn back to *sola scriptura,* the Bible, as their source of truth. Nowhere in Scripture did they find that a person is saved by good works or through God's church.

The church plays a role in proclaiming the good news, but salvation does not come through the church or its teachings. Good deeds will not accomplish a single thing toward one's salvation. The reformers realized it is through grace, and grace alone, that a person is saved. This wasn't a new concept. Jesus taught this truth to believers while He was on earth, (John 3:16).

Unfortunately, from approximately the sixth century until the early sixteenth century, the teaching of grace was not prominent and salvation by grace was not being fully taught in the church. There was no real assurance of one's salvation. Salvation by grace through faith had become muddied. Because people didn't have assurance that they would go to heaven when they died, they relied on the false security of good works and obedience to the church as a protective measure for their souls. But they never knew if they had completed enough good works! And they also never knew if the bad things they were doing diminished or counteracted their good works. This is still true today.

The reformers concluded there is no real assurance of salvation if salvation is contingent upon a person's good works.

Christians have bargained with God since the church was first established: "If I just do one more good thing, I will find favor with God and earn my way into heaven" has become their mantra. This method works for modern Christians until they are cut off on the freeway; then, all of a sudden, the good things they have done vanish with a flip of the "finger." How certain are these folks of their eternal security in such moments? Are they even thinking about eternal things?

The reformers concluded there is no real assurance of salvation if salvation is contingent upon a person's good works. These men of God accepted the fact that the Bible teaches what became known as *sola gratia* (grace alone). People are saved solely by grace, not by any attempts at good works. Good works are important to do, and we should always try to bring good into the world, but we need to understand that our good works cannot get us into heaven. However, our good works should flow from the grace we have received to help others and bring blessings to the world for Christ.

One of my favorite actresses is Julie Andrews, who played Maria in *The Sound of Music*. When Captain Von Trapp fell in love with Maria, her character was so shocked and love-struck that she burst out in song: "Nothing comes from nothing, nothing ever could! So somewhere in my youth, or childhood, I must have done something good!"

> *People believe if they help the poor, make blankets for the homeless, or feed the hungry, they will receive some sort of award or brownie point. The problem is, this is not what the Word of God teaches in regard to salvation or grace.*

Maria believed, as do many people, that if she just did something good, more good things would follow. People believe if they help the poor, make blankets for the homeless, or feed the hungry, they will receive some sort of award or brownie point. They believe any blessing or positive occurrence in their life is a direct result of previous acts of kindness. Now there is some truth to this principle, for it is a universal principle as we discover in the Bible that we reap what we sow (see Galatians 6:7-9;

2 Corinthians 9:6; James 3:18; Psalm 126:5; Proverbs 11:18 and 22:8; and Hosea 10:12-13). However, the problem is, this is not what the Word of God teaches in regard to salvation or grace and coming into relationship with God.

Years ago, when I was working in youth ministry, I attended a conference in Orlando, Florida, with about 450 other youth pastors and leaders from around the country. One of the leaders asked how many pastors in attendance believed that human beings are basically good and can find their way to God. Of the pastors who were present, 448 hands went up.

The leader responded, "Whoa! Well, how many of you believe that we are basically evil, that we are depraved in our sin?" (See Ephesians 2:1-9).

All people, before accepting Jesus Christ, are dead in their sin.

Only two hands went up.

I'm not exaggerating; I was there and one of those two hands that went up was mine. Do you want to know why? Because I knew how wicked I had been. I knew the wretchedness of my own soul without Christ. I knew how selfish I could be. I knew how bad I was before Christ and how bad I was after Christ, but by His grace, Jesus took away my wretchedness and He made me a new creation in Him (2 Corinthians 5:17).

That conference was back in the mid-1980s, but Paul addressed this same topic almost two thousand years ago in Ephesians chapter 2. He declared to the Ephesians: "As for you, you were dead in your own transgressions and sins" (Ephesians 2:1 NIV). All people, before accepting Jesus Christ, are dead in their sins.

The Prophet Isaiah addressed this issue of performing good works and trying to earn God's favor in the Old Testament. Isaiah the Prophet writes: "You come to the help of those who gladly do right, who remember Your ways. But when we continue to sin against them, you are angry. How then can we be saved? All of us have become like one who is unclean, and all our righteous acts are like filthy rags; we all shrivel up like a leaf, and like the wind our sins sweep us away." (Isaiah 64:5-6 NIV). When Isaiah said our righteous acts "are like filthy rags" before the Lord, it is a vivid picture.

This language would not make for a popular message in churches today! However, it is the Word of God. These "filthy rags" were referring to cloths that women used during their menstrual cycle. Now do you get the picture? Good works and righteous deeds before God's grace are like filthy rags before Him. Think about that for a moment.

Yes, there are many wonderful people around the world. But the Bible says even the most "wonderful" people fall short of God's perfection.

Paul agrees with Isaiah. He wrote that "all have sinned and fall short of the glory of God" (Romans 3:23, NIV). In our own minds, we may think we are good. And yes, there are many wonderful people around the world. But it is clear in the Bible that even the most "wonderful" people fall short of God's perfection.

Common Grace

Common grace is God's graciousness that He has bestowed on everyone, everywhere, all the time. It is grace God has extended to the entire world.

In the Bible we read that the sun rises and sets on both the righteous and the unrighteous (Matthew 5:45). All people have the ability to perform good deeds. Even though every person on earth is by nature totally depraved and a sinner, God has written His Law on mankind's conscience; therefore, we know right from wrong (Romans 2:15). People are wired to want to do good works.

Common grace does not save anyone, however. It doesn't set people free from the depravity of their souls. It does one of two things: It either draws people to seek after God through Jesus and His goodness, mercy and grace, or it leads people away from God to self-sufficiency, with an attitude such as, "There is no need for God, for I really am my own god."

Remember, Paul was clear in Ephesians 2 that all people are dead from the transgressions that they used to live by when they followed the ways of the world. Paul wrote that before Christ, believers lived among those who followed the ways of the world: "All of us also lived among them at one time, gratifying the cravings of our flesh and following its desires and thoughts. Like the rest, we were by nature deserving of wrath" (Ephesians 2:3 NIV).

> *Deep down in our souls, we realize we are imperfect, messed up, and broken, even if we are successful. We know we miss the mark (the definition of sin). How are people to deal with their sinful nature so that they might be set free from it and come to know God?*

Though this is not easy to swallow, *sola gratia* is one of the Big 5 of our faith.

Deep down in our souls, if we are truly honest with ourselves, we realize we are imperfect, messed up, and broken, even if we are successful. We know we miss the mark (the definition of sin). We know we have sinned. How are people to deal with their sinful nature so that they might be set free from it and come to know God?

Jesus alone (*solus Christus*) is able to save by the work He did on the cross and through His resurrection. How is this appropriated to individual people? How is someone able to receive this work of Christ on the cross? How are they able to receive forgiveness of sin?

Only by grace (*sola gratia*).

Effectual grace is the unmerited favor of God bestowed upon people to be forgiven of their sins so they might be born again, saved, and able to come into a relationship with God through Jesus Christ and His work on the cross.

Effectual Grace

There is another type of grace called effectual grace, also known as saving grace or special grace. Effectual grace is when unmerited favor is given from a superior to one of lower nature or stature.

All people are in a place of lower stature compared to God. The New Testament takes this concept even further and presents grace as a special gift from God for the salvation of undeserving sinners who can do nothing to earn God's favor or salvation.

In other words, effectual grace is the unmerited favor of God bestowed upon people to be forgiven of their sins so they might be born again, saved, and able to come into a relationship with God through Jesus Christ and His work on the cross.

Grace allows a person to know their sin is forgiven because of Jesus alone, not because of anything they have done. In his book *Grace*, Max Lucado writes:

God's grace has a drenching about it, a wildness about it, a white-water riptide attorney upside-downside about it. Grace comes after you. It rewires you from insecure to God-secure, from regret-riddled to better because of it. From afraid to die, to ready to fly. Grace is the voice that calls us to change and then gives us the power to pull it off. It's all about grace. Oh how God desires us to know his grace.[27]

What a beautiful picture of God's grace in our lives, and it is a gift to you and me!

Paul says that because of God's great love, He has extended grace. Love for whom? For you!

Sola Gratia: Grace Alone

How is grace received?

After coming to an understanding and acceptance of the fact that all people have sinned and fall short of God's glory (Romans 3:23), the question is: How does a person receive God's grace?

The answer is found in Ephesians 2: "But because of his great love for us, God, who is rich in mercy, made us alive with Christ even when we were dead in transgressions—it is by grace you have been saved" (Ephesians 2:4-5 NIV).

Paul says that because of God's great love, He has extended grace. Love for whom?

For *you.*

It can't be any clearer. There is no mention of feeding the less fortunate, serving at church, or cleaning someone's house or helping the poor, for one's salvation, although we should all be doing these wonderful acts. It's as if God says, "Thank you, but no extra-points." You are saved by grace alone, *sola gratia*.

The doctrine of *sola gratia* was affirmed very early in church history. Just a few short years after Jesus's death and resurrection, as the church was growing, a debate ensued as a result of Paul's work with the Gentiles.

> *It is God's choice, through His great love and mercy, that He extends grace for salvation through Jesus Christ alone.*

Many Gentiles (non-Jews who were coming to faith in Jesus) and Jewish believers (the Messianic Jews who believed Jesus to be their Messiah) were coming to faith in Jesus. The Jewish believers were upset that the Gentiles were coming to their Messiah, but were not being physically circumcised. The fledgling church called a council of the church leaders to discuss and debate this dilemma. At the council, Peter stood up and said:

"Now then, why do you try to test God by putting on the necks of Gentiles a yoke that neither we nor our ancestors have been able to bear? No! We believe it is through the grace of our Lord Jesus that we are saved, just as they are" (Acts 15:10-11 NIV).

Peter acknowledged that circumcision was a burdensome yolk for the Jews that never saved anyone. He declared it is only by God's grace and because of His love for humanity that anyone is saved. It is God's choice, through His great love and mercy, that He extends grace for salvation through Jesus Christ alone, *solus Christus*.

Grace is first received through the work of the Holy Spirit. Without the Holy Spirit working in people's hearts, they are not able to receive Jesus.

As Paul wrote to the Romans, "But God demonstrates his own love for us in this: While we were still sinners, Christ died for us" (Romans 5:8 NIV). God loves us so much that He sent His own Son to die for us, and pours out the Holy Spirit to enable us to receive this gift of grace.

To the Ephesians, Paul wrote: "For it is by grace you have been saved, through faith—and this is not from yourselves, it is the gift of God—not by works, so that no one can boast" (Ephesians 2:8-9 NIV). Grace is then received only through faith. Paul taught that this faith is a gift "not from yourselves, it is the gift of God."

Grace is first received through the work of the Holy Spirit. Without the Holy Spirit working in people's hearts, they are not able to receive Jesus. The Holy Spirit convicts people of sin and continues to woo people until they ask Jesus into their life. This is the gift of grace.

If I had a gift for you, how would you receive that gift? Normally, you would put your hands out. It would be terrible for me to take the gift back once I had offered it. God never does that. This is the greatest news in the world!

> *God's amazing grace saves, makes righteous, justifies, redeems, and makes new…It helps people extend that same love, mercy, and grace to others who needs God's love and grace. It helps God's people live a life full of Christ.*

Do you know what the best part is? Grace is a gift and all we have to do is receive it! It is that simple. In fact, people believe they must have to do something, but this is not what is taught in the Word of God. A person only has to receive the gift. This is the good news of Jesus Christ.

God's amazing grace saves, makes righteous, justifies, redeems, and makes new. This grace helps people live for Jesus and it helps them live daily in this grace. It helps people extend that same love, mercy, and grace to others who need God's love and grace. It helps God's people live a life full of Christ.

John Newton was raised in a Christian home. His father was the captain of a ship. His mother was a godly woman who constantly prayed for him. When he was only seven years old, his mother died. Bitterness entered John Newton's heart and he began rebelling against God and life. His father put John into the sea trade, and he began to be known and feared as one who blasphemed God all the time.

When someone is foul-mouthed, we say he has "the mouth of a sailor." Even the sailors feared Newton's blasphemy and bad language. They believed God's wrath would come upon them if they associated with him too much. John Newton sank so low that he became a slave trader. He had no problem collecting people, fellow human beings, who had a different color of skin, chaining them, and then shipping them to the new Americas to sell as slaves.

Because of sin, no one can approach God; but because of the shed blood and death of Jesus, and by His grace, there is a way.

In John's testimony, God arrested him and he saw how wretched he was for his hatred toward God and other human beings. He received the gift of amazing grace and came to know Jesus Christ as his Lord and Savior, being forgiven of all his sins. John Newton left the slave trade, became a minister, and ended up writing many of the beautiful hymns sung in churches today. One of his most famous hymns is "Amazing Grace":

Amazing grace! How sweet the sound,
That saved a wretch like me!
I once was lost, but now am found,
Was blind, but now I see.

'Twas grace that taught my heart to fear,
And grace my fears relieved;
How precious did that grace appear
The hour I first believed!

Through many dangers, toils and snares,
I have already come;
'Tis grace hath brought me safe thus far,
And grace will lead me home.

Because of sin, no one can approach God; but because of the shed blood and death of Jesus, and by His grace, there is a way.

Max Lucado writes that as men and women prepare their hearts to receive this grace, they should know that "God has enough grace to pardon every sin, solve every dilemma, wipe every tear, and answer every question. It's more than we deserve, greater than we imagine, this amazing grace."[28]

Sola gratia, grace alone for one's salvation, redemption, forgiveness, and inner peace! This is the third of the Big 5! Have you received this special gift?

WORKBOOK

Chapter Five Questions

Question: In what ways have you tried to accomplish good works to gain favor with God? Did you ever feel as if you had done enough? Why or why not? How has reading this book given you a new freedom to accept God's free gift of grace?

_____

_____

_____

_____

_____

_____

_____

_____

_____

_____

_____

Question: Because people didn't have assurance that they would go to heaven when they died, they relied on the security of good works and obedience to the church as a protective measure for their souls. They did not understand *solus Christus*—in Christ alone—or *sola gratia*—grace alone is our salvation. How have you seen such a focus on works in churches? In what ways have you placed works and church over Jesus in your own life?

_____

_____

_____

_____

_____

_____

_____

_____

_____

_____

Question: Many believe that any blessing or positive occurrence in their life is a direct result of previous acts of kindness. Do you perform good works expecting good things in return? Do you think God blesses you based on how much you have done? Why or why not?

_____

_____

_____

_____

_____

_____

_____

_____

_____

_____

_____

Question: Jesus alone, *solus Christus,* is able to save by the work He did on the cross. How is someone able to receive this work of Christ on the cross? How are people able to receive forgiveness for sin?

_____

_____

_____

_____

_____

_____

_____

_____

_____

_____

Question: What do you need to do to receive God's grace? What will you do differently as you reach out to others?

_____

_____

_____

_____

_____

_____

_____

_____

_____

_____

_____

Action: The Bible teaches what became known as sola gratia, or "grace alone." People are saved solely by grace, not by any attempts at good works. Deep down in their souls, people realize they are not perfect and are messed up. They know they miss the mark and that they have sinned. God's amazing grace saves, makes righteous, justifies, redeems, and makes new. His grace helps people live for Jesus, and it helps them live daily in this grace. It helps people extend that same love, mercy, and grace to others who may not measure up to our own standards. It helps God's people live a life full of Christ. Ask God to help you live daily in His grace.

Chapter Five Notes

CHAPTER SIX

Only by Faith

For it is by grace you have been saved, through faith—
and this is not from yourselves, it is the gift of God.
*— **Ephesians 2:8** (NIV)*

For in the gospel the righteousness of God is revealed—
a righteousness that is by faith from first to last, just as
it is written: "The righteous will live by faith."
*— **Romans 1:17** (NIV)*

Now faith is confidence in what we hope for and
*assurance about what we do not see. — **Hebrews 11:1***
(NIV)

I recently visited a neighbor who asked me to come
for a visit. This neighbor, a faithful Jewish man, was
struggling inside. He was facing an upcoming surgery
and was terrified. During our visit he asked me, "How
can I really know God?"

Many people ask this question. It's one of the most
important questions anyone can ask.

The following testimony is from an important figure in history, who also wrestled with this question, "how is one saved?"

It's the year 1515, and I have been struggling for years about my faith in God. Oh, I have taught theology in the New Testament at the University of Wittenberg, but I could not come up to you with a clear conscience of my sinfulness and my guilt. I even went to Rome and crawled up hundreds of stairs on my knees to try and rid myself of unrighteousness, but alas, it did not leave me. Here I am a theologian, yet ravaged in my soul toward God, a righteous, holy God and myself. Oh when I think of God who is holy and righteous, I cringe inside, and now I am teaching on Paul's letter to the Romans.

I felt that I was a sinner before God with an extremely disturbed conscience. I could not believe that God would placate me. There was nothing I could do to satisfy the righteousness of God!

As I read this letter, the words "righteous" and "righteousness" grab my attention, and I hate it. Whenever I read and teach on Romans 1:17, I despise it! For God says through Paul, "In it the gospel in righteousness of God is revealed." What is this righteousness? I can't obtain it! But this righteousness from God is revealed, "a righteousness that is by faith from first to last just as it is written, 'the righteous will live by faith.'" I can't do this! Oh, I hate that phrase "righteousness of God," which, according to custom for all the teachers, I had taught.

> *"The righteous shall live by faith." There I began to understand that the righteousness of God is that by which the righteous lives by a gift of God, namely by faith!*

I had been taught to understand philosophically regarding the formal or active righteousness, as they call it, with which God is righteous and punishes the unrighteous sinner.

Though I lived as a monk without reproach, I felt that I was a sinner before God with an extremely disturbed conscience. I could not believe that God would placate me. There was nothing I could do to satisfy His righteousness! I did not love—yes I even hated—the righteous God who punishes sinners, and secretly, if not blasphemously, certainly murmuring greatly, I was angry with God, and said, "As if, indeed, it is not enough, that miserable sinners, eternally lost through original sin, are crushed by every kind of calamity by the law of the Ten Commandments, without having God add pain by the gospel and also by the gospel threatening us with his righteousness and wrath!" Thus I raged with a fierce and troubled conscience. Nevertheless, I beat importunately upon Paul at this place, most ardently desiring to know what St. Paul wanted.

At last, by the mercy and grace of God, meditating day and night, I gave heed to the context of the words, namely from Romans 1:17, "In it the righteousness of God is revealed, as it is written, 'The righteous shall live by faith.'" There I began to understand that the righteousness of God is that by which the righteous lives by a gift of God, namely by faith! And this is the meaning: the righteousness of God is revealed by the gospel, namely, the passive righteousness with which merciful God justifies us by faith!

And suddenly I felt for the very first time in my life that I was altogether born again and had entered paradise itself through open gates. There a totally other face of the entire Scripture showed itself to me. Thereupon I ran through the Scriptures from memory. I also found in other terms an analogy, as, the work of God—that is, what God does in us, the power of God, with which he makes us strong, the wisdom of God, with which he makes us wise, the strength of God, the salvation of God, the glory of God, *is by faith—and I was forever changed.*

> *And suddenly I felt for the very first time in my life that I was altogether born again. I had entered a paradise itself through the open gates...*

And I extolled my sweetest word with a love as great as the hatred with which I had before hated the word "righteousness of God." *I now loved it!* Thus that place in Paul was for me truly the gate to paradise. *Because He gave me and made me righteous not by my works but by faith.*[29]

Who penned these profound words that describe such a radical heart transformation? Martin Luther, the father of the Protestant Reformation.

Hopefully, his testimony affirms what most people struggle with in their quest to know God. Luther's own revelation of being made righteous, the revelation of being justified by faith in Jesus Christ, and the revelation of Christ's work on the cross became the foundation of the reformed faith.

Luther's own revelation of being made righteous, the revelation of being justified by faith in Jesus Christ, and the revelation of Christ's work on the cross became the foundation of the reformed faith.

Now let's continue on the journey of understanding the Big 5 of our Faith.

So far we have learned the first three doctrines:

- *Sola scriptura*: Faith is found on the authority and sufficiency of Scripture alone.
- *Solus Christus*: In Christ alone is our salvation.
- *Sola gratia*: People are saved by grace alone.

Now we move to the fourth truth, one that goes hand in hand with sola gratia: *sola fide*, by faith alone.

What Exactly Is Faith?

A little child stands at the edge of a pool. Her daddy is waiting in the water for her to jump in. "You can jump! Daddy will catch you!" he coaxes. But fear grips the little girl; her dad can see it in her eyes.

He encourages: "You can do it! You can jump! Have faith in Daddy!"

"But I will drown!" she cries, thinking she will sink to the bottom if she jumps in.

"Just jump," her dad says. "I will catch you, sweetheart!"

All of a sudden, she looks at her father, closes her eyes, and jumps into his arms. She doesn't sink. She doesn't drown. And it wasn't blind, because she saw her daddy. That is faith.

> *Faith defined is pretty simple. Faith is a belief or a trust in someone greater than oneself. The Bible says faith is a gift from God.*

Faith defined is pretty simple. Faith is a belief or a trust in someone greater than oneself. In the Bible we discover that faith is a gift from God (Ephesians 2:8).

Three Elements to Faith

1. Saving Faith, *Sola Fide.*

The most important element of faith is called "saving faith," or *sola fide* in Latin. *Sola fide* literally means, "By faith alone we are saved."

Saving faith is the special gift given by the Holy Spirit for one's salvation in Jesus. This special faith flows from the gift of grace to believe and put one's trust in Jesus and all He did for us on the cross for our sins, guilt and shame, and belief in the resurrection and the forgiveness of sin for our salvation.

Sola fide deals with the same key question asked in the previous chapter on grace: How are people saved and how do they become followers of Jesus?

During the time of Martin Luther and the reformation in the 1500s, the Roman Catholic Church had taught that a person could only be saved by the church and the teachings of the church, accompanied by good works and belief in Jesus and grace. Luther states how the Roman Catholics viewed faith: "They fall into error [about faith], saying, 'Faith is not enough; one must do works in order to be righteous and be saved.'"[30] This was the tension Martin Luther wrestled with for years until the Holy Spirit revealed to him the biblical truth about righteousness, grace, and faith. As we've learned, the reformers came to realize that salvation comes only through God's free gift of grace through faith.

Remember, grace is the special gift from God for the salvation of undeserving sinners who can do nothing to earn God's favor or salvation. How is this grace and salvation appropriated in someone's life? Through faith alone: *Sola fide*.

Faith is a living, daring confidence in God's grace, so sure and certain that a man would stake his life on it a thousand times. Martin Luther

Because faith was so miraculous and real to Martin Luther, he defines faith very descriptively, stating:

> Faith is a divine work in us. It changes us and makes us to be born anew of God (John 1); it kills the old Adam and makes altogether different men, in heart and spirit and mind and powers, and it brings with it the Holy Spirit. Oh, [faith] is a living, busy, active mighty thing, this faith; and so it is impossible for it not to do good works incessantly...Faith is a living, daring confidence in God's grace, so sure and certain that a man would stake his life on it a thousand times. This confidence in God's grace and knowledge of it makes men glad and bold and happy in dealing with God and all His creatures; and this is the work of the Holy Spirit in faith.[31]

This is the saving, living faith God has for all who will receive it as a gift.

2. Daily Living Faith.

The second element of faith is what I call "daily living faith." Christians have to learn to live by faith for their entire lives, not just to receive salvation. Living by faith makes the description of faith found in the book of Hebrews real: "Now faith is confidence in what we hope for and assurance about what we do not see" (Hebrews 11:1 NIV).

> *Biblical faith is not blind trust in the face of contrary evidence. It is not an unknowable "leap into the dark," rather, biblical faith is a confident trust in the eternal God who is all-powerful, infinitely wise, and eternally trustworthy.* David Chapman

Dr. David Chapman of Covenant Seminary clarifies what biblical, daily-living faith is:

> Defining faith as "assurance" and "conviction," the author [of Hebrews] indicates that biblical faith is not a vague hope grounded in imaginary, wishful thinking. Instead, faith is a settled confidence that something in the future—something that is not yet seen but has been promised by God—will actually come to pass because God will bring it about. Thus biblical faith is not blind trust in the face of contrary evidence. It is not an unknowable "leap into the dark," rather, biblical faith is a confident trust in the eternal God who is all-powerful, infinitely wise and eternally trustworthy—the God who has revealed Himself in His Word and in the person of Jesus Christ, whose promises have proven true from generation to generation. It is belief in a God who will "never leave nor forsake" His own. (Hebrews 13:5).[32]

This is the biblical definition and description of how faith works in a Christian's daily life. We need to learn to have faith in God in all areas of our lives, not just for salvation. We should live by faith in the workplace. We should have faith that each day God will guide us in our studies at school, in our marriage, and/or in raising our children. If retired, we should have faith and hope to continue to do great things in the latter part of life for God. It's a living faith.

People with living faith are confident of God's presence and of His plans. A person with this kind of faith begins every day knowing that God is for them and not against them (Romans 8:31-32). God's promises are true and the Word teaches those who are faithful will walk and stand on those promises. It's daily faith in a living and good God and serving Him in all areas of our lives. And when we do, we see miracles happen!

Without the special gift of faith, the other spiritual gifts, like the gifts of healings and gifts of miracles...cannot function.

3. The Special Gift of Faith.

The third element of faith is what I call "the special gift of faith." This kind of faith is mentioned in 1 Corinthians 12. The Apostle Paul writes:

> *Now there are a variety of gifts, but the same Spirit...To one is given the word of wisdom through the Spirit, and to another the word of knowledge according to the same Spirit; to another faith by the same Spirit; and to another gifts of healing by the one Spirit, and to another the effecting of miracles, and to another prophecy; and to another distinguishing of spirits, to another various kind of tongues, and to another the interpretation of tongues. — 1 Corinthians 12:4, 8-10 (NASB)*

One of the Holy Spirit's gifts is a special gift of faith. Without the special gift of faith, other spiritual gifts like the gifts of healings, gifts of miracles, and other charismatic gifts cannot function. This faith trusts God for what others may believe to be impossible. It's the foundation for all the other gifts of the Spirit, allowing them to flow and function for the building up of the body of Christ. This faith sees miracles happen.

People had faith in Jesus, not faith in the religious acts or faith in the miracle. They had faith in Jesus to do the miracle.

This was the kind of faith seen while Jesus was ministering on earth. People had faith in Jesus, not faith in the religious acts or faith in the miracle. They had faith in Jesus to do the miracle. The Bible lists testimony after testimony of people who were healed after coming to Jesus by faith.

One example was a woman with the issue of bleeding. She had given all of her money away in an attempt to be healed, but nothing had worked. However, she believed in Jesus's power to heal. So she pushed her way through the crowd, reached out and touched just the hem of His robe, and indeed she was instantly healed. Jesus made it clear that she was freed from her disease because of her faith (Mark 5:25-34).

This is where God wants all Christians to be living on a regular basis. God wants His people to believe in Him for miracles every day. Matthew records Jesus talking with His disciples, whom He had given authority over demons and sickness. In one episode, the disciples couldn't seem to heal a young boy. Jesus gave the reason for their inability to perform the miracle: "Because you [the disciples and not the boy or the boy's father] have so little faith" (Matthew 17:20 NIV).

Jesus continued, "I tell you the truth, if you had faith even as small as a mustard seed, you could say to this mountain, 'Move from here to there,' and it would move. Nothing would be impossible" (Matthew 17:20 NLT).

Jesus never condemns believers for doubting, but He rebukes believers, especially the leaders, for unbelief.

Matthew is telling us that even if a Christian's faith is only the size of a mustard seed, Jesus can still use this tiniest seed of faith to perform miracles.

Jesus never condemns believers for doubting, but He rebukes believers, especially the leaders, for unbelief. (Remember, "there is therefore now no condemnation for those who are in Christ Jesus" [Romans 8:1 NKJV].) God sees doubt in the believer's heart, but He also sees the tiny seeds of faith. Learning and receiving this truth is powerful, and Jesus tells us why: "Everything is possible for one who believes" (Mark 9:23 NIV). Anyone who believes in Jesus and His almighty power faces no impossibilities. This is the special gift of faith that every believer can walk in.

Saving faith saves us from sin and death. When an unbeliever realizes his or her need for salvation and is convicted by the Holy Spirit for his or her sin, the Holy Spirit continues to move in the heart of that person. As we learned in the previous chapter, it is by grace alone that the believer is saved, and through faith, this salvation is manifested in the new Christian's life.

Taking a step of faith and believing that Jesus Christ died on the cross for sin is what saves a person. Believing this is the only way to be totally forgiven from sin and cleansed from all our mistakes, guilt, and shame, so we can be given eternal life. Once we are born again, we begin to learn living by faith daily. Then we are given special faith to see God do miracles in our lives and others'.

> *By grace alone the believer is saved, and through faith, that salvation is manifested in the new Christian's life.*

In discovering the three elements of faith, a question comes to mind: What does faith in Jesus do for us besides save us?

Saving Faith Leads to Righteousness

Sola fide makes the believer righteous, or made "right with God." This is what Martin Luther struggled with. Luther was trying to be righteous in his own strength by trying to do good works and by helping the poor. But deep down he knew it wasn't working. It wasn't until he studied Romans 1:17. While preparing his lecture to teach on the passage, he finally understood this wonderful gift. He realized it was by faith alone that he had been "made right with God."

> *Being righteous doesn't mean there won't be times of failure. But when followers of Jesus confess their sin and ask Jesus to be Lord of their life, they enter into the right relationship with God.*

As a result of Jesus's work in our hearts, we are then able to help others and give glory to God because of His righteousness. Being righteous doesn't mean there won't be times of failure. That will happen—just as it happens in any relationship. But when followers of Jesus confess their sin and ask Jesus to be Lord of their life, they enter into the right relationship with God.

Including Romans 1:17, the Apostle Paul writes in a couple of other passages about us being made righteous. He writes, "For just as through the disobedience of the one man [Adam] the many were made sinners, so also through the obedience of the one man [Jesus] the many will be made righteous" (Romans 5:19 NIV). And to the Corinthians he says, "God made him [Jesus] who had no sin to be sin for us, so that in him we might become the righteousness of God" (2 Corinthians 5:21 NIV).

Because of Jesus's obedience, even to the point of suffering and death on the cross, we are made righteous with God in His sight, because of faith. What wonderful news!

Saving Faith Justifies

Saving faith not only saves us from sin and makes us righteous; it also *justifies* us.

> *Jesus changes people from the inside out and sets them free from whatever is holding them back.*

Everyone has been around somebody who constantly tries to justify his or her actions. Believing in Jesus and His work on the cross justifies believers, so they no longer have to go around trying to justify their choice of lifestyle. Jesus changes people from the inside out and sets them free from whatever is holding them back. Jesus justifies us!

Justification means "just as if I had never sinned." What does this mean? We don't have to try and do things to feel justified—we strive internally to make sure God loves us and has forgiven all our sins! We are justified by faith in the work of Jesus Christ on the cross. God looks at us sinners through Jesus and sees us as His sinless children. Through the shed blood of Jesus on the cross, God sees His children cleansed, purified, and made righteous. He justifies them to be in a relationship with Him. This is one of the most miraculous things in the universe.

Saving Faith Gives Assurance

Sola fide also gives us the assurance of our salvation. I have counseled many Christians through the years who questioned their salvation. Even more have questioned if they can have assurance of their eternal life with Jesus. It is more common among Christians than we would believe.

It is important to help us have an assurance of our salvation. Without it, the devil can play mind games with us, causing us to fear and fall back into trying to do enough "good works" to be saved, made righteous, and be justified. We have already revealed this to be impossible without grace and faith, which are gifts from God.

I write these things to you who believe in the name of the Son of God so that you may know that you have eternal life.

One of the best ways to have an assurance of our faith is go to the Word of God and have faith in the Word. Let's look at just a few passages. I want to encourage you to not just read them, but pause and meditate on each verse to come to a new assurance of your salvation:

Yet to all who did receive him [Jesus], to those who believed in his name, he gave them the right to become children of God—children born not of natural descent, nor of human decision or a husband's will, but born of God. — John 1:12-13 (NIV)

And this is the testimony: God has given us eternal life, and this life is in his Son. Whoever has the Son has life; whoever does not have the Son of God does not have life. I write these things to you who believe in the name of the Son of God so that you may know that you have eternal life. — 1 John 5:11-13 (NIV)

*Very truly I tell you, whoever hears my word and believes Him who sent me has eternal life and will not be judged but has crossed over from death to life.
— John 5:24 (NIV)*

*All those the Father give me will come to me, and whoever comes to me I will never drive away. ... Very truly I tell you, the one who believes has eternal life.
— John 6:37, 47 (NIV)*

*I give them eternal life, and they shall never perish; no one will snatch them out of my hand. — **John 10:28 (NIV)***

*For you did not receive the spirit of slavery to fall back into fear, but you have received the Spirit of adoption as sons [and daughters], by whom we cry, "Abba! Father!" The Spirit himself bears witness with our spirit that we are children of God — **Romans 8:15-16 (ESV)***

*For I am convinced that neither death nor life, neither angels nor demons, neither the present nor the future, nor any powers, neither height nor depth, nor anything else in all creation, will be able to separate us from the love of God that is in Christ Jesus our Lord. — **Romans 8:38-39 (NIV)***

*And you also were included in Christ when you heard the message of truth, the gospel of your salvation. When you believed, you were marked in him with a seal, the promised Holy Spirit, who is a deposit guaranteeing our inheritance until the redemption of those who are God's possession—to the praise of his glory. — **Ephesians 1:13-14 (NIV)***

*For it is by grace you have been saved, through faith— and this is not from yourselves, it is the gift of God. — **Ephesians 2:8 (NIV)***

To him who is able to keep you from stumbling and to present you before his glorious presence without fault and with great joy—to the only God our Savior be glory,

*majesty, power and authority, through Jesus Christ our
Lord, before all ages, now and forevermore! Amen.*
— *Jude 1:24-25 (NIV)*

In all of these passages and many others, we have an
assurance of our salvation. It's not because of what we
have done, but because of what God the Father has done
through His Son Jesus, and by the Holy Spirit! And if we
have faith in the Word of God (*sola scriptura*) and
receive Jesus and His work on the cross by grace through
faith (*sola gratia* and *sola fide*), then we can have the
assurance of our faith and salvation for eternity!

Saving faith in the work of Christ and His Word gives
us the assurance of our salvation.

How to Live by Faith

We have discovered in this chapter that the Christian
is made righteous by faith, for the righteous live by faith.
Christians recognize that they can't do it on their own.
They need the Holy Spirit. They need His grace, and
they must choose it daily. They know it is impossible to
please God without faith (Hebrews 11:6). It's a different
mindset. Living by faith is a daily choice, but the results
are miracles.

*The Bible promises the Word is near to
God's people.*

The Bible promises the Word is near to God's people. It is in their mouths and in their hearts (Deuteronomy 30:14). This is the word of faith God wants proclaimed:

"If you openly declare that Jesus is Lord and believe in your heart that God raised him from the dead, you will be saved. For it is by believing in your heart that you are made right with God, and it is by openly declaring your faith that you are saved. As the Scriptures tell us, 'Anyone who trusts in him will never be disgraced.'" (Romans 10:9-11 NLT).

WORKBOOK

Chapter Six Questions

Question: We read an excerpt from Martin Luther in which he agonized about his own lack of righteousness in faith. How have you agonized over your faith? How has God revealed to you that you are loved by Him?

_____
_____
_____
_____
_____
_____
_____
_____
_____
_____
_____

Question: How do you demonstrate a living faith in your everyday life? How do you handle difficult circumstances in life? In what ways has your faith been tested? How has God been faithful to you?

_____
_____
_____
_____
_____
_____
_____
_____
_____

Question: Describe a time when you trusted God for what others may have believed to be impossible. Have you ever witnessed a miracle? If so, please describe.

_____
_____
_____
_____
_____
_____
_____

Question: How does your faith make you "right with God"? Do your good works improve your faith? Why or why not?

_____
_____
_____
_____
_____

Question: In what ways do you choose faith daily? Are you consistent in your choices? How will you strengthen your faith?

_____
_____

_____
_____
_____
_____
_____
_____
_____
_____
_____
_____

Question: How can you have an assurance of your salvation? Is having a saving faith enough? List some of the Scripture verses that give you assurance of your salvation.

_____
_____
_____
_____
_____
_____
_____
_____
_____
_____

Action: Biblical faith is a confident trust in the eternal God, who is all-powerful, infinitely wise, and eternally trustworthy. It is trust in the God who has revealed Himself in His Word and in the person of Jesus Christ, and whose promises have proven true from generation to generation. Taking a step of faith and believing that Jesus Christ died on the cross for sin is what saves a person from sin and death. Believing this is the only way to be completely forgiven from sin and cleansed of all mistakes, rebellion, selfishness, and pride. As a result of

Jesus's work in the hearts of believers, we are then able to help others and to give glory to God because of His righteousness. Ask God to show you how He can use you to help others.

Chapter Six Notes

CHAPTER SEVEN

All Glory to Him

Whatever you do in word or deed, do all in the name of the Lord Jesus, giving thanks through Him to God the Father. — Colossians 3:17 (NASB)

An athlete is interviewed by a reporter after winning an important game and responds by saying, "Well, first I want to thank the Lord Jesus Christ for the talent He has given me, because without Him I wouldn't be here today." Every so often, a famous actor or singer will give praise to God upon winning an Oscar, or Emmy or a CMA award.

These famous public figures give praise and glory to God on TV, but in all honesty, most people watching are probably wondering how sincere they really are. Was their praise to God ever genuine? Whether it was or not, they gave glory to God for their accomplishments. This leads us to the last doctrine of the Big 5, which answers the age-old question: What is the primary purpose of human beings?

God wants people to enjoy life and the gifts He has given, but people's main purpose is to glorify the Creator in every area of life and to enjoy Him and His creation.

According to the Westminster Confession of Faith's Shorter Catechism, God's purpose for human beings is "to glorify God and enjoy Him forever!"[33] People have been created with this purpose. God wants people to enjoy life and the gifts He has given, but people's main purpose is to glorify the Creator in every area of life and to enjoy Him and His creation.

Adopting this attitude toward life changes things. Dr. Gregg Strawbridge writes that "the Reformation reclaimed the scriptural teaching of the sovereignty of God over every aspect of a believer's life."[34] He contended that the reformers realized they were created to glorify God in all that they did because He was sovereign over all.

When we acknowledge God's sovereignty and understand that we are created to glorify God in all we do, we begin to live for Him rather than for selfish motives. Throughout the Middle Ages, the concept that permeated society and culture was the notion that some things are sacred and everything else is secular. The church was on the sacred side, and the world was on the secular side, which was really the evil side. Although there was a sense of the sacred in some of the arts and education, there was still a view of the secular to some degree.

This view has expanded more in the twenty-first century as the secularists have militantly demanded the separation of so-called "church and state" in all arenas of life. Along with this, the Church today has abdicated her role and influence of the government and has even joined this view of separation of sacred and secular, which has not been a positive change in our society.

What happened during the Reformation has baffled both Christian and non-Christian historians.

What happened during the Reformation has baffled both Christian and non-Christian historians. They struggle to pinpoint how society began to change so quickly, first in Europe and then in the parts of the New World that later became the United States. This mindset of the sovereignty of God began to permeate the entire society. Songs were written about God—even bar songs! Artists began lifting up God, drawing and painting religious art.

Soon came a revival in education. It was no longer only for the wealthy; education was available for all people. This impacted the economy; entrepreneurialism took off. Godly politicians began to transform failing governmental systems. The middle class also rose to prominence during the Reformation. Society was changing, and one reason was due to the teachings of *soli deo gloria.*

In returning to the historical understanding of *soli deo gloria*, with the Reformation, people began to see that everything God created is good and should be used for the good of others and for God's glory.

Soli Deo Gloria: For the Glory of God

These developments encouraged the birth of the last doctrine in the Big 5: *soli deo gloria,* which means "for the glory of God alone." For centuries, the Christian church grew in its understanding of this concept, and God's people directed attention to God and His sovereignty.

> *Society, not just the church, needs a new reformation. This country needs a great awakening that will reclaim the arts, business, and government for the Kingdom of God.*

But in the last 150 years or so, Christians have moved away from this concept of *soli deo gloria* to a more secular belief system, which is man-centered and ultimately leads to corruption.

Society, not just the church, needs a new reformation. This country, the United States of America, needs a great awakening that will reclaim the arts, business, and government for the Kingdom of God, and not in a "theistic" way. God is calling men and women of righteousness and integrity to influence school systems, the business world, medicine, entertainment, and even politics. This happens when people embrace the mindset and truth of *soli deo gloria*—for the glory of God alone in all things.

Soli Deo Gloria Defined

The shortened explanation of *soli deo gloria* is "in all we say and do, give glory to God!"

The Apostle Paul wrote in Colossians 3:17, "Whatever you do in word or deed, do all in the name of the Lord Jesus, giving thanks through Him to God the Father" (NASB).

> *There are three areas of our life in which we can give glory to God: in salvation and Christian life, in our public life, and in our private life.*

This phrase "whatever you do" means quite simply to do everything in the name of the Lord Jesus Christ in order to bring glory to God the Father. Paul taught this throughout his letters. In 1 Corinthians 10:31, a debate had surfaced about the freedom of a believer. One issue was whether a believer could eat meat that had been sacrificed to idols if he had been invited over for a meal at a friend's house who was an unbeliever. Was that wrong?

Paul was acknowledging that this was a very real issue for many people. He taught that, as a Christian, we have freedom in what we eat and drink, even if we go to a non-Christian's home for a meal. We are to show the love of Christ to them, be a light for them, and glorify God in how we act. Today, we may be invited to a non-Christian's home for a meal or a party, and it may not be "food sacrificed to idols," but it could be a party where there is a lot of worldly behavior happening. How should we act? Do what Paul said to do: "So whether you eat or drink or whatever you do, do it all for the glory of God" (1 Corinthians 10:31). However, if you sin or act inappropriately, it does not glorify God, does it?

I am ministering in Africa where some of these similar practices and issues that Paul was addressing to the early church are affecting Christians and churches today. The pastors I am teaching have struggled with whether it's right or wrong to attend funerals or meals where meat has been offered to ancestors (pagan worship) and now is being served to the people. But through God's grace, wisdom, teaching sound biblical doctrine, and teaching *soli deo gloria,* God has done some amazing things to bring peace, unity, understanding, grace, and freedom to the churches.

How can we give glory to God in our life? There are three areas of our life in which we can give glory to God:

- In salvation and our Christian life
- In our public life (family, friends, and work)

- In our private life

> *Not everyone is called to be a pastor, but everyone is called to be a minister, whether in the workplace, the home, or a neighborhood.*

1. Glorify God in Salvation and Our Christian Life

When a person comes to Christ, their salvation gives glory to God. As a matter of fact, Jesus says it in Luke 15:10 (NIV): "There is rejoicing in the presence of the angels of God over one sinner who repents." When someone is born again, all of heaven rejoices and glorifies God's goodness, grace, and mercy. When we share our testimony of how Jesus saved us or other stories of God's mercy in our lives, people are touched and God is glorified!

When we become a Christian, our lives are changed and we begin to live a new way: God's way. People begin to see a difference in our lives: how we talk, how we dress, how we act or don't act, how we care, and how we love and want the best for others. We become a representative or an ambassador for Christ (see 2 Corinthians 5:16-21). So we are called to live for Christ and glorify Him in all that we say and do.

Paul writes in Ephesians 2:10 that the reason God has saved His children by grace through faith is because "we are God's handiwork, created in Christ Jesus to do good works, which God prepared in advance for us to do" (Ephesians 2:10 NIV). God has a work for each of us to complete for His glory!

For this reason, Paul exhorted, "As a prisoner for the Lord, then, I urge you to live a life worthy of the calling you have received" (Ephesians 4:1 NIV). Every Christian is called by God to be a minister, whether in the workplace, the home, or the neighborhood. Not everyone is called to be a pastor (Glory to God!), but everyone is called to minister to others and be a witness through their life. This is another foundation of the reformed faith. It is the priesthood of every believer as found in 1 Peter 2:9:

"But you are a chosen people, a royal priesthood, a holy nation, God's special possession, that you may declare the praises of him who called you out of darkness into his wonderful light."

We are to live for God as Christians and we have a role to show and share our story with all those we come in contact with. Are we living as God desires us to live as followers of Jesus?

2. Glorify God in Our Public Life (Family, Friends, and Workplace)

This second way to glorify God really continues from the first way, as a Christian. Our public life includes our family and friends, but also our workplace and all the other venues we participate in, including some of the Internet "Big 5" like Facebook, LinkedIn, Instagram, Twitter, Google+, and other online social media.

Family and friends should know we are a follower of Jesus. This does not mean we always talk about Jesus and our faith, or worse, beat them over the head with the Bible and being "self-righteous". But we should just live our lives as Jesus did: loving, caring, serving others, healing, and showing the way to God. Even on social media, our family, friends, coworkers, neighbors, and others should see us living differently (not weirdly) while being full of joy or at least living in peace. They should see in us a supernatural peace and a hope that doesn't make sense by the world's standards.

Practically, as Christians we should speak words that build up and encourage, not tear down and wound. We honor our spouse as Christ honors the church. We should teach and raise our children in the Word and the ways of Christ. And we should be a light in a dark world. Doing these things exhibits the life of Christ to others.

> *Believers' attitude, character, and integrity when their boss is directly in front of them should be the same as when he or she is not around.*

God even gives instruction in His Word for how to behave in the workplace:

> *Slaves, in all things obey those who are your masters on earth, not with external service, as those who merely please men, but with sincerity of your heart, fearing the*

Lord. Whatever you do, do your work heartily, as for the Lord rather than for men, knowing that from the Lord you will receive the reward of the inheritance. It is the Lord Christ whom you serve. — **Colossians 3:22-24 (NASB)**

Don't get caught up on the term "slaves" here, in today's understanding we could make it to be employees. The Apostle Paul was talking to Christians and exhorting them to obey and respect those who were over them. Believers' attitudes, character, and integrity when their boss is directly in front of them should be the same as when he or she is not around. This brings glory to God. We should try to have the attitude to do everything with "all your heart," for the Lord and not for the approval of people. What a great work ethic!

First and foremost, live by grace. No one can do anything of eternal significance by his or her own strength. Love God and serve and love people by grace.

When I was attending the local public high school, we had several Christian coaches. One coach, who was leading the Fellowship Christian Athletes that I was a part of, gave several of us football players a booklet called *Total Release Performance* by Wes Neal. One of the major points I learned from this booklet was that, as a Christian athlete, I needed to give my all (my total release performance) and do my best by playing for an audience of one: Jesus Christ and the glory of God.[35]

That little booklet changed my thinking forever. From that point on, I didn't play my best for my parents in the stands (even though I was glad they were there), and I didn't play my best for my girlfriend cheering me on (although it was nice to know she was cheering for me). I began to play sports and try to do everything in life to glorify Jesus. Isn't this what *soli deo gloria* is about?

Johann Sebastian Bach said this: "The aim and final end of all music should be none other than the glory of God and the refreshment of our soul!"[36] Bach understood *soli deo gloria*. He even signed this phrase on almost every piece of music, and if there was not enough room, he simply wrote *"SDG."*[37] Amazing! Are we living our public life like this?

3. Glorify God in Private Lives

According to Proverbs 15:3, "The eyes of the LORD are everywhere, keeping watch on the wicked and the good." This verse alone should cause a Christian to ask: How am I in my private life? Am I different on Sunday morning at church with my fellow Christians than I am the rest of the week? Am I glorifying God in my life when no one is around?

"Character is doing the right thing when nobody's looking."

It is so easy to fall back into the ways of the world. But by God's grace, we can live holy and pure lives, even when in private. We can live for God's good and glory each day.

Several years ago, I heard about a survey regarding the television viewing practices of pastors when they were at a conference. The percentage of "adult TV" was higher than the average business group staying for a conference. What this reveals is that many pastors don't glorify God in their private lives. It grieves the Lord and damages our witness for Christ.

J. C. Watts, a great University of Oklahoma football player and a former U.S. Congressman, once said: "Character is doing the right thing when nobody's looking. There are too many people who think that the only thing that's right is to get by, and the only thing that's wrong is to get caught."[38] This definition of character helps us to understand that what we do in our private life matters, especially to God. Therefore, do we glorify God in our private lives, when no one is looking?

How to Live for the Glory of God

First and foremost, live by grace. No one can do anything of eternal significance by his or her own strength. Love God and serve and love people by grace. Otherwise, our motives become selfish.

Living for the glory of God allows His love to be poured out to others.

Second, ask these questions: Will this action or speech glorify God? Will cheating on this test glorify God? Will cutting corners in business to make an extra buck glorify God? Will disrespecting a spouse glorify God? Will disrespecting others glorify God? Will rebelling against your parents glorify God? Asking these questions help to change attitudes and stop negative behavior.

Third, acknowledge evidence of God's goodness in your life. When something good happens, give praise to God for allowing it to happen, like the famous singer or athlete who points to God as the means for their great success.

Acknowledging God's goodness and truly living for *soli deo gloria* results in loving God well. This love allows the Christian to see people in a new light, as God sees them. Even though God may see the sin in a person; He sees a broken heart. He sees the displaced child, or the hurting mother. He sees the pain of the drug addict. He sees the loneliness of shunned. Living for the glory of God allows His love to be poured out to others and see others as God sees them. This is *soli deo gloria.*

Chapter Seven Questions

Question: How do you glorify the Creator? How do you enjoy Him? Are these new concepts for you? Why or why not?

_____

_____

_____

_____

_____

_____

_____

_____

_____

_____

Question: What does it mean to glorify God in salvation and in your walk? How is God calling you to give glory to Him in your personal walk as a "minister"?

_____

_____

_____

_____

_____
_____
_____
_____
_____
_____
_____
_____
_____

Question: What areas of your private life do you need to change so that God can be glorified? What changes in your attitude do you need to make? Would your close family members be able to say you glorify God in your home all the time?

_____
_____
_____
_____
_____
_____
_____
_____
_____
_____
_____

Question: "Whatever you do in word or deed, do all in the name of the Lord Jesus, giving thanks through Him to God the Father" (Colossians 3:17 NASB). Does everything you do in your daily life, including your words, actions, text messages, and social media, give glory to God? If not, what can you do in your daily life to change this?

_____
_____
_____
_____

_____

_____

_____

_____

_____

_____

Action: God wants His people to enjoy life and the gifts He has given. But man's main purpose is to glorify the Creator in every area of life and to enjoy Him and His creation. In Christians' personal salvation, they give glory to God. But they can also give glory to God in their Christian walk. Everyone is called to be a minister, whether in the workplace, the home, or a neighborhood. The Christian can live for God's good each day, even in private. Do everything with "all your heart," for the Lord and not for the approval of man. Serve people and love God by grace. Ask this question: Will this action or speech glorify God? Acknowledge evidence of God's goodness in your life. Acknowledging God's goodness and truly living for *soli deo gloria* results in loving God well. Living for the glory of God allows His love to be poured out to others.

I would encourage you to take time to read the following passages to get a fuller understanding of how we should live in our public and private lives:

- Matthew 5:1-20, 33-47; 6:1-4, 19-34; 7:1-27
- Luke 10:25-37
- John 13:1-20; 14:12
- Romans 8:1-17, 28-39; 13:1-15:7
- Ephesians 4:17-5:21

This is not an exhaustive list about living our lives differently than the world for the glory of God, but these will challenge us to think more about how the Lord desires us to live by His grace through the Holy Spirit.

Chapter Seven Notes

_____

_____

_____

_____

_____

_____

_____

_____

_____

_____

_____

_____

_____

_____

_____

_____

_____

_____

_____

_____

_____

CONCLUSION

Foundations of Faith

Therefore, dear friends, since you have been forewarned, be on your guard so that you may not be carried away by the error of the lawless and fall from your secure position. But grow in the grace and knowledge of our Lord and Savior Jesus Christ. To him be glory both now and forever! AMEN. — *2 Peter 3:17-18 (NIV)*

These are the Big 5 of our faith: *sola scriptura, solus Christus, sola gratia, sola fide,* and *soli deo gloria.* An understanding of these five doctrines is important to maintaining direction, consistency, and solid adherence to the truth as revealed by God.

The principle of *sola scriptura* is the very basis of Christian theology. Scripture functions as the most foundational guide believers have, providing them with knowledge of God's character as well as instructions on Christian living and faith.

The consequences of failing to trust in Scripture as the true and inspired Word of God can include overreliance on human doctrine and philosophies instead of God's truth. This tendency toward human works and deceptions can be observed in history, particularly when certain church traditions and teachings diverged from complete reliance on the Scriptures by prioritizing some of its own rules, interpreting the Word based on preconceived beliefs. However, the Protestant reformers reestablished the truth that acknowledgement of and belief in the authority of the Scriptures is essential to the Christian faith.

While good works are essential in the life of a Christian who loves God and wishes to please Him, it is impossible to earn salvation.

Those who believe in the truth of the Scriptures will also believe that what they say about grace and the One who gives it is true. It is only by grace, *sola gratia*—through Jesus Christ and only Christ, *solus Christus*—that one can be delivered from sin. God provides a single way to be saved from spiritual death; it is a gift for all and it is up to the individual to receive or reject it. Either way, Jesus Christ is the only way to receive it.

While it is by grace that believers are saved, it is through faith that they receive grace and therefore salvation, righteousness, and justification. According to the Scriptures, good works are not sufficient to save us. While good works are essential in the life of a Christian who loves God and wishes to please Him, it is impossible to earn salvation. According to the tenet of *sola fide*, we are justified only after we have committed our lives to Christ through faith.

The fifth and final principle is *soli deo gloria*: striving to do everything, whether in private or among others, in such a way as to bring glory to God. The purpose of this is to bring both believers and nonbelievers closer to Christ, as well as to give God the worship and honor that He deserves. This requires consistency and integrity within the life of the believer; full commitment to Christ is key. This principle encompasses all meaning and purpose in the lives of believers.

The Big 5 are the foundation upon which all matters of the Christian faith are built. Those who live by these truths will be the followers of Christ who reflect the character of God to the world. And these transformed lives represent the new reformation the church needs now.

To him who is able to keep you from stumbling and to present you before his glorious presence without fault and with great joy—to the only God our Savior be glory, majesty, power and authority, through Jesus Christ our Lord, before all ages, now and forevermore! AMEN.
— Jude 1:24-25 (NIV)

REFERENCES

Notes

1. Stanley J. Grenz, David Guretzki, and Cherith Fee Nordling. "Indulgences," in *Pocket Dictionary of Theological Terms* (Downers Grove, IL: InterVarsity Press, 1999).
2. Steven Ozment. *The Age of Reform 1250-1550* (New Haven, CT: Yale University Press, 1980), 208.
3. James White. *Scripture Alone* (Minneapolis, MN: Bethany House, 2004), 27—8.
4. Ibid., 28.
5. Martin Luther. *Luther's Works*, Vol. L.xvii.580, quoted in J. H. Merle D'Aubigne, *History of the Reformation of the Sixteenth Century*, vol. 2, trans. H. White (London: Religious Tract Society, 1846), 245.
6. White, *Scripture Alone*, 41—2.
7. Benjamin B. Warfield. *The Inspiration and Authority of the Bible,* edited by Samuel G.

Craig. (Phillipsburg, NJ: The Presbyterian and Reformed Publishing Co., 1948), 296.

8. "Of the Holy Scriptures." In *Westminster Confession of Faith and Catechisms, in Modern English*, Chapter 1.4 (Livonia, MI: Evangelical Presbyterian Church, 2010), 4.

9. *The Belgic Confession,* Article 3. Protestant Reformed Churches of America. Accessed 5 July 2015. http://www.prca.org/about/official-standards/creeds/three-forms-of-unity/belgic-confession.

10. *Ibid.* Article 7.

11. Josh McDowell. *Josh McDowell Answers Five Tough Questions* (Wheaton, IL: Tyndal House Publishers, 1991), 49—51. Also quote from James I. Packer, *Fundamentalism and the Word of God* (Grand Rapids: Eerdmans, 1958), 78. In addition, I have added my own thoughts within the citation by Josh McDowell. However, most of the work in this section is by Josh McDowell.

12. John Calvin. *Institutes of the Christian Religion: 1559,* ed. John T. McNeill, trans. Ford Lewis Battles. *The Library of Christian Classics*, vols. 20 and 21 (Philadelphia: The Westminster Press, 1960), I.viii.1, 82.

13. Ralph Reed. *Awakening: How America Can Turn from Economic and Moral Destruction Back to Greatness.* (Brentwood, TN: Worthy Publishing, 2014)

14. The following three major keys to Bible study are known as Inductive Bible Study Method. The

following sections have been derived from my personal studies from seminary, but also using two major books I used for this work.

15. Kay Arthur. *How to Study Your Bible* (Eugene: OR: Harvest House Publishing, 1994), 23.

16. Gordon Fee and Douglas Stuart. *How to Read the Bible for All Its Worth* (Grand Rapids: Zondervan Publishing, 2003), 30.

17. *Ibid.,* 23.

18. Stuart Townend and Keith Getty. "In Christ Alone my Hope is Found." Thankyou Music, 2001. http://www.stuarttownend.co.uk/song/in-christ-alone/.

19. Andreas J. Kostenberger. "Commentary Notes on the Gospel of John." In *ESV Study Bible* (Wheaton, IL: Crossway Publishing, 2008).

20. Donald McLeod. "The Person of Christ." In *Contours of Christian Theology*, edited by Gerald Bray (Downers Grove, IL: InterVarsity Press, 1998), 17.

21. Martin Luther. "Earliest Christian Creeds," quoted in John J. Davis, *Handbook of Basic Bible Texts* (Grand Rapids: Zondervan, 1984), 61.

22. John J. Davis. *Handbook of Basic Bible Texts* (Grand Rapids: Zondervan Publishing, 1984), 68—9.

23. *Ibid.* Note, this list is not an exhaustive list of Scripture, and I have added several passages as well.

24. C. S. Lewis. *Mere Christianity* (New York: HarperCollins Publishing, 2001), 51.

25. Josh McDowell, "Trilemma (Lord, Liar, Lunatic?)." Accessed November 2, 2015, http://www.josh.org/resources/apologetics/videos /.

26. C. S. Lewis, *Mere Christianity*, 52.

27. Max Lucado. *Grace: More Than We Deserve, Greater Than We Imagine* (Nashville, TN: Thomas Nelson Publishing, 2014).

28. *Ibid.*

29. Testimony taken from J. Pelikan and H. Lehman, eds., *Luther's Works: American Edition, 55 vols.* (St. Louis: Concordia; Philadelphia: Fortress Press, 1955–1987), vol. 34, 237–238. Note: the author has paraphrased some of Luther's testimony to help with the context and enhance the reader's experience of the testimony, which has been italicized.

30. *Ibid.*, p. xiv.

31. Martin Luther. "Introduction." In *Commentary on the Epistle to the Romans*, translated by J. Theodore Mueller (London: Oliphants, LTD., 1954), xiv—xv.

32. David W. Chapman. "Commentary Notes on Hebrews 11:1-5." In *English Standard Version Study Bible* (Wheaton, IL: Crossway Publishing, 2008).

33. "The Shorter Catechism," Section 1. In *Westminster Confession of Faith and Catechisms, in Modern English* (Livonia, MI: Evangelical Presbyterian Church, 2010), 2.

34. Gregg Strawbridge. "The Five Solas of the Reformation." Essay for Audubon Drive Bible Church, Laurel, MS, 1993. Accessed August, 1, 2014, http://www.fivesolas.com/5solas.htm.

35. Wes Neal. *Total Release Performance* (Grand Island, NE: Crosstraining Publishing, 2000).

36. Calvin R. Stapert. "To the Glory of God Alone." In *Christian History*, issue 95, 2007. Accessed August 1, 2014, http://www.christianitytoday.com/history.

37. *Ibid.*

38. J. C. Watts. *BrainyQuote.com*, 2015. Accessed July 6, 2015, http://www.brainyquote.com/quotes/quotes/j/jcwatts106082.html.

About the Author

Daniel Gilbert, Ph.D. (University of Aberdeen) is passionate about the transformative power of God to help people enter into a deeper relationship with God. He has a zeal for teaching theology and sound doctrine in a way that makes it real and practical. As a pastor, theologian, international speaker, author, ministry consultant, and coach, Dr. Gilbert is dedicated to teaching biblically based principles to empower people to go deeper in God, grow stronger in life, and go higher in their destiny.

Dr. Gilbert and his wife, Mary Beth, are the founders of EmPowered Living International Ministries, a ministry to help educate, equip, and EmPower leaders to transform communities through sound theology and humanitarian action. Through EmPowered Living, Dr. Gilbert has founded ELIM Theological Institute in Siaya, Kenya educating pastors to transform their communities for Christ. In addition, they are helping with several humanitarian projects in Africa, including special projects for orphanages, schools and villages.

Dr. Gilbert's new radio program, "EmPowered Living with Dr. Gilbert," airs on Voice of Hope Radio – Africa teaching his Bible and Theology courses to spread the Good News and sound doctrine throughout the great Continent of Africa.

He also is the President of Soterian USA, the non-profit subsidiary of Soterain Group, Ltd. a corporation building cost-effective and high quality hospitals and medical care in East Africa.

Having been in ministry for over 30 years, Dr. Gilbert has pastored in Aberdeen, Scotland; Hampton Roads, Virginia; and Los Angeles, California. He has served as Professor of Theology and Church History and the Dean of Students at The King's University and also is currently an Adjunct Professor for Regent University and The King's University.

Daniel has been married to his college sweetheart, Mary Beth, since 1985, who is an international women's speaker. They are blessed to have their precious daughter, Maria. They currently reside in Los Angeles, California.

For more information about having Dr. Gilbert or Mary Beth Gilbert speak at your conference, church or retreats, contact his office at: 213-973-2011 or email him at DrGilbert@empowered-living.org. Visit EmPowered Living International's website for more information at www.empowered-living.org.

About Sermon to Book

SermonToBook.com began with a simple belief: that sermons should be touching lives, *not* collecting dust. That's why we turn sermons into high-quality books that are accessible to people all over the globe.

Turning your sermon series into a book exposes more people to God's Word, better equips you for counseling, accelerates future sermon prep, adds credibility to your ministry, and even helps make ends meet during tight times.

John 21:25 tells us that the world itself couldn't contain the books that would be written about the work of Jesus Christ. Our mission is to try anyway. Because, in Heaven, there will no longer be a need for sermons or books. Our time is now.

If God so leads you, we'd love to work with you on your sermon or sermon series.

Visit www.sermontobook.com to learn more.

62223096R00090

Made in the USA
Lexington, KY
01 April 2017